Doublelife

One Family, Two Faiths and a Journey of Hope

Harold Berman
&
Gayle Redlingshafer Berman

Longhill Press, New York

Authors' Web site and blog: www.doublelifejourney.com
J-Journey Web site: www.j-journey.org

Cover design by Errol Wahlhaus – errol@graphicki.com
Cover photo by Zev Rothkoff – www.zevrothkoff.com

ISBN: 0-6157-2115-X
ISBN-13: 9780615721156

Every event described in these pages really happened. In a few cases,
names of certain people have been changed.

Acclaim for Doublelife

An inspiring story of the Jewish tradition's capacity to move souls and to change lives. The thunderbolt conclusion will keep you thinking for days ...

Daniel Gordis
Award-Winning Author of *The Promise of Israel*

Doublelife captures what it means to find your true soul. Every interfaith couple, indeed every spiritual seeker should read this remarkable story.

Rabbi David Aaron
Bestselling Author of *The God Powered Life*

Doublelife is a moving and engaging story of a couple who found love – and their destiny – embracing the Jewish faith and each other. Told in an accessible format that reveals its authors charming personalities, *Doublelife* is a book that will speak to anyone with an open mind and a big heart.

Hannah Brown
The Jerusalem Post's Film Critic & Author of
If I Could Tell You

This is a sacred story – an achingly beautiful story. I was touched and moved many times over while reading it. In truth, I didn't want to let it go from the very first page. The writing is so true, so authentic, so real and alive. There is so much that is profound, so much that is heart-warming, so much we all have to learn from the Bermans' journey

Susan Vorhand
Author of *The Mosaic Within*

Contents

Prologue

Sometime around March each year – the date varies according to the Hebrew calendar – strange goings-on take hold of Jewish communities around the world. Children don costumes as if it were Halloween, minus the monsters and ghosts. With their parents, they march off to synagogue, sitting raptly at attention to the sing-song intoning of the Book of Esther. Each time the reader happens upon the name *Haman*, the youngsters awake from their silence and raucously wave noisemakers – called groggers – in the air.

To the casual observer, the scene makes no sense, though the part with the groggers, at least, can be easily explained. In the story, Haman is the King's assistant who almost succeeds in his plot to wipe out the Jews of the kingdom. He is the story's personification of evil, and so his name must be symbolically erased.

But what of the rest – the costumes and why this obscure Biblical story is publicly read in the first place? Purim – the name of this Jewish holiday – is all about what we can't see, what hides beneath the surface just beyond our vision. The book of Esther tells a story of undiscovered identities, dual roles, words that take on meanings beyond the obvious. The book struggles between the poles of fate and destiny, what life thrusts on us versus the choices we make. In the story, God never makes a direct appearance, yet is always present. Underneath the surface, this is no children's holiday.

Even the book's name is a hint – in Hebrew, *Megilat Esther* simply means the Scroll of Esther. But the words *Megilat Esther* yield another meaning: to reveal that which is hidden. The Book of Esther is a book of secrets.

Esther is also a book of interfaith marriage, one of the secrets the story's heroine keeps even from her husband. Esther, the Jew, marries the Gentile King Ahasuerus, putting her in the ideal position to save her people from the wicked Haman. Some have interpreted the story as a Biblical endorsement, offering ancient proof that two faiths within one marriage not only works, but can be a positive societal force.

To stop there, however, is to linger on the surface as the real story unfolds beneath. Interfaith marriage is more than shuttling back and forth between two sets of holidays. It is about coming to terms with who you are – in public, in private, and in those deep recesses of the soul you may not acknowledge even to yourself. It is about understanding where your partner is coming from, and then trying to understand where she is *really* coming from. It is about the unspoken chasm that exists, and how to bridge it, or not.

The story of Esther is not merely a Biblical relic, but a story of today. In America, of those Jews who marry, one in every two intermarry. Nearly 40% of *all* married Americans wed someone of another religion, while nearly 30% of American adults are practicing a different religion from the one of their childhood.[1]

Behind these mammoth statistics lay stories – stories of faith lost and found, of hope abandoned and reclaimed, of confusion and clarity, of boundaries shattered and brick walls hit. Attached to the statistics, of course, are the obvious stories, the kind the media likes to tell – how to negotiate Christmas and Hannukah, Easter and Passover, and the like. And then there are the stories underneath the stories, the hidden secrets, the people behind the costumes.

These stories are not merely about the individual, but about the paths the couple does – and does not – walk down together. Many of these stories – the stories underneath the stories – are not unique. They are merely untold.

Everyone has a story. This is ours.

---

1   The Pew Forum on Religion and Public Life.

Part I
Where to Begin? At the Beginning …

All journeys have secret destinations
of which the traveler is unaware.

Martin Buber

May 22, 1989

Dear Gayle,

I hate blind dates. I had always envisioned spotting the woman of my life across a crowded room. We would have a long courtship. After say, six months or a year, I would propose in some idyllic spot. The woman of my life would be swept away by emotion, and we would joyfully contemplate our future together over tears and champagne.

OK – I've watched too many movies. But we did get the tears and champagne. Showing up on your doorstep and asking you to marry me after we had met just three times, and had known each other for only a week after the blind date I didn't want – that part I couldn't have imagined.

And you still said yes! Please don't misunderstand me. I know deep down that this is exactly right. It's just that I can't figure out how we got here.

I'm not the impulsive type. I don't rush into things – except maybe an occasional appliance purchase. I usually review a choice over and over. I write down lists of pros and cons. I cover the same ground again and again. I look before I leap.

But not, apparently, when it comes to one of life's most important decisions. My mind still reels when I try to grasp how an East Coast boy and a Midwestern farm girl found each other in the middle of South Texas. Beyond our shared musical lives, our backgrounds could not be more different.

So I should tell you a little more about the man you will marry. And then you can decide if this is who you thought you were marrying all along.

I was born in Passaic, New Jersey, once a thriving mill town, but a tired display of urban decline by the time I made my appearance. After a brief run in the Bronx, my parents followed the path of many in search of better schools and a better life for their children. The suburbs beckoned. In our case, that meant Monroe. Every summer, thousands escaped the stifling New York City heat and made the pilgrimage to Monroe's bungalow colonies. Seasonal houses hugged the lakes that sprawled between the Hudson River and the Catskill Mountains.

The city dwellers thought they had reached paradise. My brother and I were bored out of our minds.

So as I entered 7th grade, seeking a respite from Monroe's suburban stasis, I took up piano and clarinet and singing, all in the same year. Many kids discovered themselves on the basketball court or the football field. I sought the practice room and the stage. I did my school work grudgingly, just so I could get to the real work of playing music. Music became, and remains, my world. It was a world to which I could always retreat when life seemed hard, a world that is made for those thoughts and feelings that are so elemental that words cannot do the job. Entering that world made me feel different, even special.

Every Saturday, I took the 50-mile bus ride to "The City" to study at the Manhattan School of Music. And every summer, I lived by the shores of Lake Messalonskee at New England Music Camp near Waterville, Maine. For a shy teenager, those places were magical. They teemed with a vibrancy that eluded me in the everyday grind. The sounds of aspiring musicians that ascended from every corner – those were the sounds of prayers that cannot be spoken. The sounds of others who inhabited the same magical world, and who taught me that maybe I wasn't so different after all.

After high school, I again made my way to the City – not "The City" – but to Boston to study at the New England Conservatory of Music. In Boston, music became not a retreat from life, but life itself. I admit to not feeling the same religious intensity now, playing marches with the Air Force Band here in San Antonio. Just the same, music is magic.

And you're right – since our courtship has been so short, we now ought to take our time and wait a year before getting married. Not because of any uncertainty on your part or mine. But because everything has snowballed so quickly and we need to catch our breath.

Not that anything is going to happen in the next year except for our love growing stronger. I may have watched too many movies – but in this case, "love at first sight" could not be more real.

Love,

Harold

☙❧

May 22, 1989

Dear Harold,

You're surprised?! When my first marriage failed, I thought I'd never go down the aisle again. I could just keep dating and skip over the commitment part. Ah, the best laid plans . . .

Two weeks ago, I would have passed you by on the street without recognizing you. One week ago, I met you for the first time. Today, I cannot imagine my life without you.

One week isn't enough time to learn anything more about each other than that we belong together.

So here's a little about my sordid past.

I grew up on a farm in Central Illinois. Acres of crops separated us from our nearest neighbors, and when we said we were going to "The City," we meant Peoria.

While my friends who lived in town were going to each other's homes to play jacks or hopscotch or Monopoly, I discovered other childhood pleasures. After school, I would ride my horse, Star, at a canter past the sweet-smelling cornfields, and the not-so-sweet-smelling pig pen. Whenever I felt down, I could always count on a ride in the fresh county air to lift me up.

Music and I have been together all my life. Sometimes, if I was really upset, I would sing to Star as I rode, or would play the piano, and all cares would vanish. As they say, music is the soul's own speech.

I have never felt closer to God than when I am singing arias from Handel's Messiah or Mozart's Requiem. But I also know that the talents God gave me are not for religious music alone. There would be a great big hole in my life if I weren't also singing opera. I can't imagine not singing the Queen of the Night in Mozart's "The Magic Flute," or Adele in Strauss' "Die Fledermaus."

I could never marry a man who did not understand music, or appreciate the long, demanding hours of practice or the pressures of performance. Strange, though, that singing is so much a part of my life, and you haven't even heard me sing. Then again, it's only been a week. I hope you like what you hear.

My ancestors on my dad's side came to the U.S. in the late 1800s. My mom's side goes back considerably further. The Van Pettens arrived in the late 1600s. Seventy-two Van Pettens served in the Revolutionary War, and my ancestors include George Read, who signed both the Constitution and the Declaration of Independence.

Farm life instilled in me the good old Protestant Work Ethic. My dad managed to run a 600-acre farm while simultaneously working at the TV and appliance stores he co-owns. Meanwhile, my mom was always busy making food for the farmers, cleaning mud off the plows, and keeping the planter and combine going while others took a break – all in the midst of raising four kids. That's why my job directing the church music program takes up about sixty hours a week, in addition to my full day of teaching music at St. Mary's University and my performing. It's in my blood to work 24/7.

"Love at first sight" – should I be wary when this is my second go-around, that I've fallen for you so quickly? Logic says proceed with caution. But love isn't logical. My heart knows it's time to go full speed ahead.

Love,

Gayle

ॐ∾ঔ

May 24, 1989

Dear Gayle,

Since you mentioned that sixty hour a week church music job, I suppose we ought to touch on the "religion thing." Not that

I think it matters. I'm Jewish. You're Christian. But I just don't see this as much of an issue.

Then again, not every day does a Minister of Music in a large Texas church marry a Jew. But I cannot imagine this being a problem. Being Jewish is who I am, but it certainly doesn't limit who I am – or who I marry.

Growing up, my family went to the Monroe Temple of Liberal Judaism. I attended Hebrew school there, had my Bar Mitzvah there, and even bucked the trend and stuck around for a few years after Bar Mitzvah. Being Jewish is important to me, but it's not something that I will allow to put up roadblocks in other areas of my life.

I believe that religion was meant to bring people together, not keep them apart. Any time religion comes between people, it is worse than useless. Since God created all people, He clearly meant for people to be together and not for religion to get in the way. I want you to know where I stand, and that I think bringing our two religions under one roof can make for an even stronger relationship.

I've met some Christians who think everyone must believe as they do. Those people scare me. But I know you're not that way at all.

Love,

Harold

৵৹

May 25, 1989

Dear Harold,

Now that we've been together – and it has been all of a week, after all – I couldn't agree more. We love each other and I don't see religion getting in the way. Yet . . .

A week ago, I never would have imagined that I would say "I do" to a Jew. My goodness, I'm the Minister of Music at Colonial Hills Church. I conduct choirs for three services every Sunday, in front of thousands of congregants. A week ago, sharing my life with a Jew would have included trying to make him a Christian.

But meeting this particular Jew has turned that idea on its head. I see in you a real connection with God. You already have a relationship with Him. But you need to know that I need my connection with God to be through Jesus, although I sense that somehow you don't have that need.

I always took Christianity seriously, and my musical and religious lives often overlapped. Every Sunday morning, we piled into the Oldsmobile to go to Sunday school and church. It was there, in the choir, that my career as a professional singer really began. By high school, I already filled in for the regular organist at my own church and at others in the area. And it was in high school that I asked Jesus to be my Personal Savior so that I would be sure to go to heaven when I died.

I continued in college, attending Bible study several times a week. I also played organ and directed choirs in churches of practically every denomination (I'm very ecumenical!). Being a musician in church works so well for me because I have to be part of the action. I could never just sit in the pew.

No matter what, I think our love will carry us through, because beyond the obvious religious differences, we share a profoundly deep connection. As a Christian, I can participate in your Jewish life, and it means a lot to me that you are willing to sing in my church choir from time to time, at least when you're not being hired to sing at other churches. We agree that God would never want to keep two people apart who love each other so much. And as my mom said when I told her about you, "Well, Jesus was a Jew."

I'm looking forward to sharing the rest of my life with you!

Love,

Gayle

☙ ❧

June 5, 1989

Dear Harold,

Remember our second date – sitting at the jazz band concert when you casually slipped your hand into mine? You are so cute. I almost felt like I was in high school.

But when you're in high school, there's no wedding to plan. When I was in high school, I had my fantasies about what my wedding would look like some day. The man of my dreams would sweep me off my feet. I would walk down the aisle of a church, saying "I do" as a minister would give us his blessing for a happy life together.

It's true, I've been swept off my feet. But we're going to have to revise the rest of my fantasy a bit. I'm assuming that a church wedding wasn't what you had in mind. I didn't have a synagogue wedding in mind either. So what if a minister and a rabbi join together to marry us? I can speak with Bill, the Senior Pastor at Colonial Hills Church. You had mentioned that there's an Air Force Rabbi on base. Maybe you can see if he's available. We've got a year, so he should be able to clear his schedule.

Love,

Gayle

అ∽

June 21, 1989

Dear Gayle,

I love the idea of a rabbi and a minister co-officiating our wedding. Our love transcends one religion, and nothing will symbolize that better than a rabbi and a minister standing together.

Unfortunately, it may not be possible, at least not with the handful of rabbis in San Antonio. I spoke this afternoon with Rabbi Schwartzman, the Air Force chaplain. The last Air Force rabbi was Conservative. Rabbi Schwartzman, who arrived just a few months ago, is Reform. So I thought we'd have a chance. Apparently, most rabbis simply don't do this. And after 45 minutes with Rabbi Schwartzman, I'm still not sure why.

The meeting got off to a great start. I barely got out that I wanted to speak with him about my upcoming wedding when he said, "Please don't say you're marrying someone who's not Jewish. Because I've already had two of those this week."

I persisted, and asked if he would be willing to take part in the ceremony. You can guess the answer. He told me that he had done that once years ago in Colorado, and was nearly run out of town by the other rabbis. By the end, though, he seemed sympathetic, and even offered to meet with us as we prepare for the wedding. But as far as the ceremony goes, the answer is still no.

This leaves us without a rabbi. Rabbi Schwartzman told me that the civilian Reform rabbis in town do not perform interfaith weddings. The Conservative rabbi obviously is out. And the Orthodox rabbi . . . I may not have mentioned that there is an Orthodox community outside Monroe, an ultra-Orthodox one in fact. I grew up seeing these people up close. I know all about their fanatical ways. They would probably burn an intermarried Jew at the stake if they could.

I asked Rabbi Schwartzman why Judaism is so opposed to intermarriage. He explained that the Jews are a small people, that it is a matter of survival. I told him I don't think we can survive very well if we close ourselves off from the rest of the world. Remembering something I heard growing up, I asked him about Ruth and Esther. Were they not intermarried?

He replied that this was hardly analogous as Esther saved her people, and Ruth converted. Hadn't thought about that.

What he said next I certainly hadn't heard before. Judaism only recognizes a Jewish marriage as one between two Jews. Something about marriage being a contract and the Jewish marriage contract binding people by the "law of Moses." I still don't understand. Jews can enter into all kinds of contracts with people who aren't Jewish.

Whatever Judaism says a Jewish marriage is or isn't, things are going to have to change. Jews and Christians are marrying more and more. It's just reality. I thought they had figured out when the Enlightenment came 200 years ago that you can't keep people shut up in ghettos. The world has a way of seeping in.

We agreed to meet again soon. I'll keep working on him. Maybe he'll change his mind once he gets to know me better and he meets you.

Love,

Harold

∂∞∞

June 26, 1989

Dear Harold,

I feel let down. Bill and Rabbi Schwartzman presiding together to help us tie the knot would have symbolized the inclusiveness of our relationship. We'll have to figure out another way to show our inclusiveness, but it will be hard to send the message as powerfully without the rabbi's co-participation.

I don't understand why a Jewish marriage contract binding people by the "law of Moses" should be limited to Jews. After all, Christianity (and even Islam) connects to Moses too. We follow the same Ten Commandments. We share the same Old Testament. I can understand why, using this argument, it wouldn't work for, say, a Hindu and a Jew to have a Jewish wedding. But when Judaism and Christianity share so much, I don't see why a rabbi and a minister couldn't acknowledge this reality by participating together. If the rabbi won't change his mind, we'll just find other ways to include Christianity and Judaism in our wedding.

By the way, Bill had a very different reaction. I was scared to death to tell him that I am marrying a Jew. He's religiously pretty conservative – and he's my boss. But my fears were unfounded. He said he didn't see why it would be a problem, and that he'd be happy to be part of our wedding in whatever role we wanted him to play. Apparently, he's not concerned that I will "leave the fold" or that our marriage will threaten Christianity's survival.

The Associate Pastor – he's a different story. Watch out. Not long ago, in a staff meeting, he proudly announced that he would be baptizing a Jew who had been attending Colonial Hills Church. He said she looked forward to becoming a "completed Jew." Thus far, he hasn't mentioned any incompleteness on your part. But we'll need to keep our guard up.

It's hard to take him too seriously, though. This is the same person who, against the staff's vocal protests and better judgment, has arranged for the church to host a "Pig-Pickin' Picnic." While a country-and-western band plays, a whole pig with an apple in its mouth will be roasted on a spit. When he suggested the band play some country songs during the church service to drum up business for the Pig-Pickin' Picnic, he was met with an immediate burst of laughter from the rest of the staff.

Each religion has its challenges. We may not be able to get a rabbi for our wedding, but I have a feeling you will never have to deal with a Pig-Pickin' Picnic in temple, even here in Texas.

Love,

Gayle

బ్కె

October 9 (Yom Kippur), 1989

Dear Harold,

I did it! I still can't believe it. And now that it's over, I'm not sure why I did it. Never did I imagine I could endure twenty-five hours without eating or drinking. When you told me that Jews fast on Yom Kippur so they can focus on the prayers without interruptions, I wanted to be supportive and share with you to the extent I could.

So when I got up yesterday, in the midst of my race to the breakfast table, I decided I would fast with you from start to finish. You called Yom Kippur the holiest day on the Jewish calendar, so it didn't feel right to ignore it.

As one hour of the service ran into the next, and the next, and the next, my stomach and I thought, "Wow – Jews starve themselves like this every year just to come closer to God." Is it because they feel they must suffer for the sins they have committed during the year, or does fasting help them connect more with God because they, like Him, are not in need of food for this one day (or so they pretend)? Or is it truly so that they can pray without interruption – there were times it seemed like the service might continue until next Yom Kippur.

I'm amazed you could sit in front of the congregation and play clarinet for the services. By the afternoon I felt light-headed and could not have thought about performing, or anything else that required much energy.

As I listened to the rabbi chanting the Hebrew prayers in the Air Force Chapel, I thought of Jesus fasting for forty days and forty nights. Forty times the hunger and weakness I experienced today is incomprehensible.

Now that it's over, I'm glad I took the plunge. Just as you felt closer to God by experiencing self-sacrifice, I felt closer to you knowing that I was sharing something important with you. Only, I haven't yet figured out what that something was.

The physical and emotional about-face at the Jewish Community Center break-the-fast was almost jarring after the preceding twenty-five hours – not only the suddenly endless supply of food, but the festive air that permeated the room after all those hours and pages of confession.

So what are services on the Sabbath like? I imagine shorter and said on a full stomach.

Love,

Gayle

જ⚬જ

October 11, 1989

Dear Gayle,

I'm amazed that you fasted. And I'm amazed that you're so positive about it. You should know that there are many Jews who don't fast, or at least don't fast completely. And for those who do, it's usually not the part of the Jewish year they look forward to the most.

Fasting on Yom Kippur and sitting through services that go on for much of the day may not be the most enjoyable way to learn about Judaism. Many people start first with something like a Passover Seder, a Friday night service, or a Bar Mitzvah. You're the first person I've met whose introduction to Judaism was to fast on Yom Kippur. I'm grateful that you did it, and I'm glad that you got something out of it. But please know that it's only one day out of 365. I'll ask Rabbi Schwartzman where we can go for a Friday night service since they don't hold any on base. After Yom Kippur, it'll be a breeze.

Love,

Harold

෴

October 27, 1989

Dear Harold,

The San Antonio Ecumenical Center will make the perfect setting for our wedding. The hall and reception area are the right size. And even if the rabbi won't be there along with Bill, the message of our wedding will come across loud and clear when people read the word "Ecumenical" on the invitation.

You know how much I would like to have a rabbi and a minister lead the ceremony together. But since that won't be possible, I can understand why you don't want Bill to do it by himself. I wouldn't feel comfortable if Rabbi Schwartzman were the only one performing the ceremony.

I think I've found a solution, and from an unlikely place. Among my students at St. Mary's University is a Professor in the Law School. He said he can ask his friend, Judge Barlow, to serve as a Justice of the Peace. Then Bill can talk, but not actually perform the ceremony. I hadn't envisioned my wedding with a Justice of the Peace, but with Bill and our own ideas, we can inject whatever religious meaning we want.

After I toured the Ecumenical Center and reserved the date, I met with one of their counselors to explore the different ways couples like us can successfully incorporate their faiths. The books we've read have been helpful, but after the rabbi's reaction and your parents not exactly embracing the idea, I wanted to speak with a sympathetic live person. And it seemed like a counselor at an Ecumenical Center, of all places, might have some experience with this.

Barbara and I spoke for an hour, but I left without any helpful ideas. She said that many interfaith couples join a Unitarian church because it's not specifically Christian. For me that would be the worst, not the best, of both worlds. We would be in a place that's not Christian and not Jewish, but that borrows just enough from both so that we'd remember what we're missing. I want to find a way for both of our faiths to co-exist side by side, not blend together to the point where neither is recognizable.

Love,

Gayle

☙❧

October 30, 1989

Dear Gayle,

I have to agree that a Unitarian church isn't what I had in mind. It would feel to me too much like going to church, while to you it would feel like you'd given up church. I'm not sure what would be the point.

As we navigate how to bring our two religions under one roof, music again provides the connection. I got a good recommendation on a temple – at church. On Sunday morning, I was speaking with David, the other paid soloist at First Presbyterian Church. He mentioned to me that he also is the cantorial soloist at Temple Beth El, San Antonio's Reform temple. And Bess, First Presbyterian's Music Director and organist, had been the Music Director at Temple Beth El for many years.

When I mentioned we were looking for a temple where we could go to a Friday night service, they both recommended we try out Beth El. By the way, when Bess found out we were engaged, in her inimitable Texas style, she said, "Oh, I know Gayle. She's a peach of a gal."

I think so too.

Love,

Harold

ॐৠ

November 4, 1989

Dear Gayle,

I've hesitated to bring this up, but there are two things we really do need to discuss. Children and Christmas trees.

At this point in my life, I don't want children, and I don't foresee that I ever will. I recognize how important children are. There always needs to be a next generation. It's just that I do not feel equipped to raise children. I think my contribution to humanity lies elsewhere.

If we were to have children, then we would have to deal with religion differently. I know that many people in our situation raise their kids in both religions, or in neither, and let them decide when they get older. To me, the idea of raising a child in two religions seems confusing for both the child and the parents. As adults who have already formed their own perspectives, we can each enjoy what the other's religion has to offer. Children, however, are blank slates. To force a six-year old to learn one thing at temple and a different thing at church, and then try to reconcile it all at home, may be a set-up for neuroses. I also wonder if a child in that situation ever feels like he is choosing one parent over the other should he later choose one religion over the other.

If we did have children, I would feel more comfortable raising a child in one religion or even in neither. As open as I am to sharing in your religious celebrations to the extent I feel comfortable doing so as a Jew, I am not yet comfortable with the idea of raising a child as a Christian.

If we don't want to have children, then we get a free pass from having to worry about any of this. I am very comfortable spending the rest of my life with you, with no little ones in the picture. I want to make sure that you are too. You have not mentioned kids, but I don't want to assume your silence to be agreement.

Christmas trees may not pose the same existential issues as do children. Nevertheless, it is an issue for me, although one where I can be flexible. For obvious reasons, I never had a Christmas tree growing up.

When I was in fourth grade, our teacher, Mr. Saylor, brought in a midget version of a Christmas tree, and earnestly told us that it was a Hannukah bush. I rushed home to tell my mother that we were missing a vital part of the Hannukah experience. She was not impressed, and waved off the whole idea by pointing out that it really was just a small Christmas tree in disguise.

Most Jews figured that out too, opting for a real Christmas tree if they wanted one. The Hannukah bush fell into the abyss of failed sales gimmicks.

We never had a Christmas tree, a Hannukah bush, or greenery by any other name in our house in December. We had a menorah. Christmas trees were what other people had.

I know it's not rational, but I'm not entirely comfortable envisioning a Christmas tree in my house. If a tree is important to you, I will find a way to become comfortable with it. You are making compromises for me, so I should do the same.

I won't let a tree come between us. But if you really do want a Christmas tree, can it be an artificial one? I can't become comfortable with a fire hazard.

Love,

Harold

᠊ᢒ᠊ᡈ

November 7, 1989

Dear Harold,

We're not going to have problems with trees or children. Long ago, I resolved that I can impact the lives of many more children if I don't have the time demands from my own. Besides, I know I was born to sing. And if I were tied down with children, my singing career would be seriously stifled. I know we will be happy, just the two of us.

You may be surprised that a church music director feels no need for a Christmas tree. I've only had two trees in my four years living in San Antonio. The first was right after I moved here. I happened to be with a member of my church choir as he was buying his tree. He insisted on buying one for me too. My friend Peggy, also my roommate at the time, beamed when I showed up porting the soon-to-be-lovingly-decorated evergreen. I bought the second one because the guy I was then dating insisted. Only later did I realize that he pushed me to buy a tree because he knew he wasn't going to get one.

I still remember my first Christmas in San Antonio, my first away from the bitter cold and snow of the Midwest. As I left Colonial Hills after the fifth and final service, the balmy midnight air belied that it was Christmas Eve. Only the tree greeted me when I returned to the apartment, as Peggy had left to be with her family.

As a child, I wanted my family to be one of those who opened their presents on Christmas Eve immediately after church. Who wants to wait through the night to see what "Santa" brought? But waking up on Christmas morning as the sun began to peek through our living room window, I was glad I still had all the fun ahead of me.

The fun didn't last long. My family descended upon the presents like grasshoppers rushing through a field of wheat. Within minutes, piles of bows and crinkled wrapping paper were strewn in heaps across the floor. All those weeks of guessing what was in those boxes under the tree, and now it was over as I retreated across the living room with my small pile of gifts.

On my first Christmas Eve in San Antonio, as I entered the silent apartment, I decided I would savor each and every gift under the tree. By opening one present each night, I could savor that feeling of anticipation, wondering what awaited me in each remaining package for as many nights as the gifts lasted. On New Year's Day, the eighth night after Christmas, I opened the last gift.

I enjoyed making Christmas last for several days. So after we're married, we can celebrate the holiday season each night for eight nights. We can light the menorah and then open a present for each of those nights – or at least have some wine – L'Chaim!

Love,

Gayle

ॐ ॐ

November 23 (Thanksgiving), 1989

Dear Harold,

It was like an audition, but this time for the very real role of your wife. On the drive up, I did just what I do before an audition – I tried to relax, focus on what was in front of me, and not become distracted by concerns about what they will think of me.

It's also helpful, before walking on stage, to take a step back and absorb the context and all of the behind-the-scenes information. I did that too. The drive to your uncle's house in Dallas passed much more quickly by reading that book on interfaith marriage your cousin recommended. Learning from the experiences of others in your family who already have gone down the intermarried path has made it much easier than if this were uncharted territory.

From the book, I learned that interfaith marriage is quite common in the Jewish community, although the sharp increase is recent. The authors say that interfaith marriage can work, but that couples need to prepare for "time bombs" – for example, issues around the birth of a child, and how to deal with "the December Dilemma." Measured against these standards, we are excellent intermarriage candidates since we've already addressed those issues.

Alas, the book offered little detail about dealing with parents and in-laws.

As we walked through the door of your uncle's house, those familiar audition feelings began to surface, clinging to me like those people who can't help but give you advice no matter how clearly you've said that you don't want it. Am I going to be good enough? By what criteria are they going to judge me? Will I be rejected no matter how hard I try?

In some auditions, they don't take you seriously because they already have someone else in mind. I wondered if the Dallas audition would be one of those, or if there was some way to convince them anyway to take me instead of their pre-determined ideal candidate.

Suddenly finding myself deep in conversation with your father, the unwanted voices gave way, and I felt surprisingly relaxed answering his questions about every facet of my background. I tried to be me and not who I thought they wanted me to be. Your mother said little, so I had no sense of how she felt. But when your father began to talk about taking up piano as an adult and once trying an organ (in this case, not the church pipe organ, but the pretend electronic home version), I knew he was trying to make a connection.

It's nice that he told you he can understand what you see in me. But it bothers me that he's concerned anyway. I hope that will go away.

Love,

Gayle

বঃ৯

November 24, 1989

Dear Gayle,

Kugel solidifies the relationship with future in-laws. Who knew?

On previous trips, that five hour drive to Dallas could never end fast enough. Five hours of flat monotony punctuated by signs for gas stations, Dairy Queens and Denny's. This time, as mile after mile of Route 35 rolled on, I didn't want the drive to end. I didn't want to arrive at my uncle's house, where my parents would be waiting, and who knows what would happen.

You were brilliant to make kugel. As brilliant as my uncle for arranging Thanksgiving dinner in Dallas, where we could all meet on neutral territory. The kugel became a symbol. It said to my parents that you accept that I'm Jewish and that you care that I'm Jewish – more powerfully than my own words could ever convey.

By the time the pumpkin pie was served, they were impressed with you. And not just because of the kugel. I know they would prefer that I marry someone who is Jewish. My uncle's intermarriage plays into their fears – Chris and Erika are two beautiful children, but my aunt and uncle are not raising them in any religion, save for a Christmas tree in December and an awareness that they have Jewish relatives. That is my parents' fear if I marry you, and my response that we don't plan to have children does not exactly give them comfort.

Their concerns are not going away. But they now can at least appreciate all of your great qualities, and see that we are happy together. My hope is that with each meeting, their fears will diminish and their bond to you will become stronger.

To be honest, I felt just as ill at ease meeting your parents when they visited last month. They haven't voiced any opposition to my being Jewish. And their concern about grandchildren isn't so acute since they already have three, and you have three other siblings. Yet, I also had that feeling of being at an audition. That's natural – they want to know who their daughter is going to marry.

As they were leaving, your mother signaled her acceptance of my religion, saying, "We have a lot to learn."

I guess all of us do.

Love,

Harold

ॐৎঔ

December 11, 1989

Dear Gayle,

"Christmas in Blue." The Air Force Band marketing geniuses have bestowed this title on the concerts we're performing all around Texas this month. Strange, no? Even I know that Christmas is red and green, official Air Force colors not with standing.

I must admit to feeling a certain aloneness during the rehearsals. Once we get past "Jingle Bells," I'm learning many of these Christmas songs for the first time. I didn't grow up with them. Yet my fellow band members all know them. For me, this is another performance. For everyone else, this is part of a tradition that stretches back to their childhood.

I've had this same feeling walking through a mall in December. I enjoy looking at the Christmas lights. Yet I am only looking. They are not mine.

In New York, it was different. Christmas was huge, but Hannukah was sizeable enough to be noticeable.

Not so here in South Texas. At the end of this morning's rehearsal, a band member who has never been north of Dallas approached me. With an earnest look, he inquired, "So tell me, how do Jews celebrate Christmas?" I smiled at his little joke – until I realized he was serious. He really didn't know.

I suspected he wouldn't get it if I said that we celebrate by eating Chinese food. "Jews don't celebrate Christmas," I said matter-of-factly.

"What do you mean, Jews don't celebrate Christmas?" The synapses were not connecting. That someone wouldn't celebrate Christmas didn't fit into his world. He eyed me suspiciously. The air hung silently. It was as if I had said that Jews don't believe in bathing. Just when the silence began to feel a bit too uncomfortable, he shrugged his shoulders and walked away.

There were so many things I wanted to say, but there was nothing I could have said that would have bridged the gap. Then I realized that I don't owe anyone an explanation. Still, I'm looking forward to being on the other side of "Christmas in Blue" and back to a level playing field.

Love,

Harold

৵৽৹

December 12, 1989

Dear Harold,

I grew up in Farmington, Illinois – population 2,800 – Christian population 2,800. And even I know that Jews don't celebrate Christmas. This band member needs to get out more.

Your sense of aloneness is natural. But it's hard for me to imagine how it feels, since Christmas was in my life from the beginning. Ironically, working in a church does give me a sense of separateness at Christmas, but in a very different way.

Because of Colonial Hills' size, we must do five Christmas Eve services to accommodate everyone. The three ministers take turns leading the services. There's only one Minister of Music, so I get to do all five. By the end of the evening, while others are thinking about what's under the tree, I'm too exhausted to think. So for different reasons, we'll both be glad when Christmas is over.

Love,

Gayle

৵৽৹

February 9, 1990

Dear Harold,

I'm not sure what to make of Temple Beth El. My main impressions are that it wasn't what I was expecting, and that my attention wandered mostly to the professional vocal quartet since I know all of the singers. I didn't feel out of place though, especially since I know that none of the quartet members is Jewish.

Nothing about the service was objectionable. It's just that, well, nothing about it moved me. I've never been to a Friday night service before. Maybe I shouldn't have expected the same depth I found in the Air Force Yom Kippur service. A once-a-year event is going to be more intense than a weekly occurrence.

Still, on Sunday mornings at church, there's a feeling of purpose. I don't think it comes from the service itself. It's a combination of the minister's sermon, which is the centerpiece of the service, and the devotion of the congregation.

The rabbi's sermon didn't interest me so much. He went on and on about whether it is ok to have religious displays on public property. I'm not saying it's not important, just that it didn't give me anything I could take and use in my life. I don't think he mentioned God once, or even what Judaism says about this issue.

As for the congregation, people stuck with their own groups. No one reached out. And there wasn't any feeling of energy. They sat there while the quartet sang, and barely participated in the prayers. It seemed like many people didn't know the prayers very well. I know why I'm not yet familiar with Jewish prayers, but I'm surprised to find Jews who aren't.

And the place was so empty. Colonial Hills is full for all three services on Sunday morning. Do Jews not go to temple regularly? If they don't, then what do they do to make Judaism part of their lives?

Love,

Gayle

❧❧

February 10, 1990

Dear Gayle,

Other than High Holidays, I haven't been to services for some time, so I had forgotten what it was like. Since I've sung in many church services in the meantime, I could see it a bit through your eyes.

Much of the service was the same as at the Monroe Temple when I was a kid. They use the same Reform prayer book. The music is similar. But I remember the Monroe Temple services being more inspiring. Maybe our rabbi's sermons were more interesting. Or maybe how I experienced this as a child is different from how I'm experiencing it now.

Unfortunately, I had many of the same impressions as you. The sermon would have made an excellent New York Times editorial. But for that, I can just buy a copy of the Times and skip the temple. You're right – ministers usually talk about some part of the Bible and how you can use it in your life. There was none of that.

As for the congregation, I agree they weren't so friendly. Hardly anyone came over to us. Whenever I've been in a church, people have always come up, asked if I'm new, welcomed me and invited me to return. We were obviously newcomers here and the group wasn't so big. I assume they want more people to pass through their doors, so it's strange that they would ignore us.

Some aspects of the service seemed like an imitation, but not a good one, of a church service. The organ music and the choir are reminiscent of a church, but it's not the same as listening to Bach. The sermon was the centerpiece, but it lacked any spiritual center. Even some of the format echoed what I've seen in church. I've read that originally, when the Reform movement broke from traditional Judaism in the early 1800s, the Reform rabbis tried to incorporate some of the Christian religious practices they saw around them in an effort to make the service more exciting. But the imitator is rarely as interesting as what he is imitating. I've only been to Reform services, so I don't know how other Jewish services differ, except that they use a lot more Hebrew.

Jews don't rush to synagogue the way Christians do to church. They incorporate Judaism into their lives in other ways. And some, truth be told, don't incorporate it much at all. Judaism, like Christianity, is a religion. But it is also a culture, an ethnicity, a people. Some Jews relate more to the culture or the sense of identifying as a Jew than they do to the religion. And that's why you didn't see the crowds that you do in church.

Then again, if a service isn't any more exciting than this, there's not much incentive to go. I'll ask Rabbi Schwartzman if he can recommend another temple.

Love,

Harold

᪣

April 3, 1990

Dear Harold,

Only two months to go. Between our two faiths and our limited finances, it's taken a lot of resourcefulness. But everything's coming together.

We've got the San Antonio Ecumenical Center for the ceremony and the apartment clubhouse for the reception. We've got the Justice of the Peace to preside and the Air Force Band members to do the music. We've got Bill to speak and some of your relatives to do readings.

All we need now are the invitations. Oh, and my dress. If I'm going to make my own dress, I really better get started.

Love,

Gayle

᪣

April 8 (Palm Sunday), 1990

Dear Gayle,

Thanks for insisting that I sing in the Fauré *Requiem*. The informality of Colonial Hills was a refreshing break from the borderline stuffiness of First Presbyterian. Then again, First Presbyterian is paying me to sing, something you didn't offer.

I hadn't realized that Colonial Hills is the church of choice for several of my fellow Air Force Band members. As the choir lined up to march in, Mike Yasenchak turned around and teased, "So what's a nice Jewish boy like you doing in a place like this?" After college, Mike spent six months studying in Tel Aviv with a French Hornist from the Israel Philharmonic. I hope to make it to Israel one of these days.

Mike's joke triggered a realization – I never actually dated anyone Jewish in high school or college. Well, there was that summer romance with Rhonda Levine at New England Music Camp. Other than that, my serious relationships have been with Christians.

I've never sought out Jewish women to date. Truthfully, it never seemed important. As I pondered why, I dug up a long-forgotten memory of one Friday evening at the Monroe Temple of Liberal Judaism.

After Bar Mitzvah, I suffered through three years of Confirmation classes. Except for the final year, with the rabbi, the only other time in my life I felt I had wasted so much time was during Air Force basic training. In the first year after Bar Mitzvah, we each created a slide show, for no other reason than that the teacher loved slide shows. Mine was about Einstein, but I can't remember anything in it about Judaism.

The teacher in the second year required us to read Erich Von Daniken's *Chariots of the Gods*, his favorite book of the moment. Even then, *Chariots of the Gods* evoked only chuckles from us. The book attempts to show how our fair planet was established by visitors from outer space. Our only discussion relating to Judaism was something about a passage in Ezekiel where he sees a wheel, which our teacher, echoing Von Daniken, enthusiastically told us was an alien spaceship.

Sometime around then, we fourteen and fifteen year olds led a Friday night service. Each class was responsible for one Friday night "family service," and because we were older, we were supposed to deliver the sermon as a group.

We pondered our options. Nothing interesting in the slideshows. Alien spaceships seemed a better fit for the comedy club. What to discuss?

We chose intermarriage.

In essence, we said that the most important thing is to marry a good person, regardless of religious background. We then opened the conversation for discussion, an opportunity most of the congregants seized to protest our impudence. Intermarriage then was still a minor phenomenon, even in the Reform movement. We had dared to approve something we were expected to condemn. Instead of the reasoned discussion we assumed would ensue, outrage was the sole reaction to our sermon.

As one congregant after another stood up to denounce our youthful foolishness for even bringing up the topic, I suddenly found myself in the position of chief defense attorney. I couldn't believe so many people could be so close-minded, and I wanted them to hear that our generation wasn't buying it.

At one point in the evermore heated back-and-forth, I blurted out, "It would be better to marry a good person who is not Jewish than to marry a Jewish American Princess."

Spontaneous gasps, followed by . . . silence.

I guess I wasn't supposed to say that – especially the Jewish American Princess part. I was such a diplomat back then.

You will not be surprised to learn that we changed no one's mind that evening. My best friend's father pulled out his wallet right after the service and gave his son five dollars as a reward for staying out of the fray.

After that, I never went looking for a Jewish date. I know that my "Jewish American Princess" comparison was based on a faulty either/or premise –in truth, there are nice people and intolerable people of all religions. I wouldn't have been opposed to dating someone Jewish. It's just that, on those few occasions when a Jewish woman and I crossed paths, there was no chemistry.

And so, I stand by my original statement – or at least its essence, however inartfully expressed – that the most important factor in any relationship is Love, regardless of religion. Love we have, not to mention personal compatibility. The rest will take care of itself.

Love,

Harold

෨ඏ

April 10, 1990

Dear Harold,

Growing up in a small town near Peoria, interfaith marriage meant that a Methodist boy was marrying a Baptist girl. For a Roman Catholic and a Protestant to exchange vows was to enter virtually uncharted territory. Such a union would send the citizens of Farmington – all 2,800 of them – into a state of shock. We sure have them beat, don't we?

As a child, I had little contact with religions other than Christianity. Our 4-H group took field trips to different houses of worship. There was a temple in Peoria, so that was our one non-Christian stop on the itinerary. I remember only that the door handles were shaped like Stars of David.

My first contact with a Jew was with Lynn, the wife of my first husband's best friend. Neither Lynn, her husband nor Jon were into Christmas, and so they coined "Heddy Crustov, Randube" as their own special greeting during December.

Lynn's father owned a drug store in Libertyville, Illinois. On Christmas Day, people flocked to it for their last minute purchases since it was the only store in Libertyville that was open. I've always adored Lynn, and though I haven't been to Libertyville in years, we've kept in touch.

My path didn't cross with a Jew again until I came to Texas. There is a member of Colonial Hills Church who is one of the mainstays of the music department. She's involved in everything – singing in the choirs, playing piano, playing in the handbell program and the recorder ensemble, and helping out with the children's music program.

So she surprised me when she said I wouldn't see her husband at church except when the children were doing something special. When I asked why, she said, "Because he's Jewish."

I should have known. Her name is Cafi Cohen.

She said it feels strange to raise their children in the church with such an obviously Jewish surname. Also, that she and her husband can't fully share in something that is such an important part of her life is sometimes hard for her. What I find encouraging, though, is that they still have a wonderfully supportive interfaith marriage, even with children.

And then there was the Jewish guy I met while running. He offered me "the moon" and he seemed really nice. There was no chemistry, though. But at that time in my life, it would have been impossible, for religious reasons, to even think about marrying a Jewish man. That time in my life was only a year ago. It never occurred to me that I might someday marry a Jew . . .'till there was you!

Suzanne, my running partner, knows a Jewish girl who comes over to play with her daughter. One day, a friend of Suzanne's saw the two girls playing together and said, "I hope you're trying to convert her." "Of course not!" Suzanne replied. "She's happy being Jewish and there's nothing wrong with that."

Until recently, I would have felt obligated to try to convert any Jew who crossed my path – all to help them so they would be guaranteed a seat on that train to heaven. I didn't meet many Jews after all, but now I realize I never did try to convert any of them. And since I've met you, I'm convinced that Jews also have a seat on the train. I don't understand how something that now seems so obvious was incomprehensible just a short time ago.

You may remember meeting Stuart McKirdy at Colonial Hills Church. He stands in the choir next to Mike Yasenchak. Stuart's father, who is a Methodist minister, believes we usually follow the religion in which our parents raised us. My parents raised me in a religious Christian home regularly attending services. And your parents raised you with a strong Jewish identity. So we each feel secure enough in our respective faiths that we can join together without feeling threatened by the other's religion. And that combination, I think, will bring a specialness to our married life. It won't be long now!!

Love,

Gayle

ๅๅๅ

May 5, 1990

Dear Gayle,

Some people say interfaith weddings can be difficult to navigate. I say some people aren't very creative. That we don't want an exclusively Jewish or Christian wedding also means that no one tradition limits us.

The typical Jewish or Christian couple shows up for a ceremony that will hardly be different from the thousands that have preceded it. They may have a say about a few details, such as the music, or the color of the bridesmaids' dresses. Other than that, the die is cast.

We, on the other hand, get to create every detail of the ceremony, from the moment our guests arrive to the moment we leave as a newly married couple. Our ceremony will represent who we are, not what others think we should do.

I like that the ceremony will be ecumenical, and that it will involve members from both of our families. We can now show all of the naysayers that it is possible for an interfaith wedding to have religious content and yet include everyone. We do not have to make the unpleasant choice between a ceremony that includes no religion and one that favors one religion over the other. Our wedding will be a model for how religion can bring people together.

The best part is that our music will be the main unifying force. I can't wait to see the looks of surprise when we turn around and sing the Adam and Eve duet from Haydn's *Creation*. For many a wedding, the reception is more memorable than the ceremony. Given the small funds we have for the reception, and the great deal of effort we're putting into the ceremony, our wedding will put the emphasis where it should be. Better that our guests remember Haydn's *Creation* than the shortcomings of the dessert.

Like you, my only regret is that we cannot get a rabbi and a minister to co-officiate. But absent Rabbi Schwartzman's participation, we'll have to make do with a Justice of the Peace. We were right to decide against hiring one of those rabbis who, for a hefty fee, will participate in practically any kind of ceremony. Beyond the expense, a Rent-a-Rabbi who flies in from who-knows-where would barely know our names and would say the same things he or she says at every other wedding they perform. A stock wedding sermon is exactly what we don't want.

Rabbi Schwartzman has softened a bit, and even has showed a little support. While he still doesn't believe that he can physically be at the wedding, we may yet have his presence. He shared the sermon he had written for his one and only interfaith wedding. We are free to use it however we wish. It speaks eloquently to love transcending all boundaries. Since Bill has agreed to say a few words, I would like to give him a copy. This will be Bill's first interfaith wedding, so he can incorporate any of Rabbi Schwartzman's ideas that he likes.

Just one more month.

Love,

Harold

&

June 3, 1990

Dear Harold,

You'd think I had never been to a wedding before. For how many hundreds of weddings have I sung or played? And here I go and say "I do" about ten minutes before I was supposed to. At least everyone laughed right along with us. And it made for all the greater contrast as we sang the Adam and Eve duet. I noticed tears on more than a few cheeks.

I was amazed when Rabbi Schwartzman's sermon came rolling out of Bill's mouth – literally word for word. So in the end, it was like a minister and a rabbi were there together after all.

What a wonderful day! Our wedding was a religious ceremony in the deepest sense, even though not specific to either of our religions. That's what I hope our marriage will be, one where love will transcend everything else.

Love,

Gayle

᙮

June 3, 1990

Dear Gayle,

I never would have anticipated that our fathers would hit it off as if they had known each other their whole lives. They were inseparable during the reception. Remarkable when you consider that my father was born and bred in the Bronx and yours has spent his life on the farm.

Maybe it's a metaphor for our marriage. Maybe the differences that everyone thinks are important, like religion and upbringing, aren't really differences at all in the face of the underlying bonds that connect us.

Love,

Harold

᙮

Part II
And Two Become One . . .

Do not go where the path may lead,
go instead where there is no path and leave a trail.

Ralph Waldo Emerson

July 30, 1990

Dear Harold,

I've had it! When Colonial Hills Church played host to a country band and a pig roasted on a spit with an apple in its mouth, words like gross, silly and a few less mild adjectives came to mind. I assumed it was a momentary diversion.

It turns out though, that the Pig-Pickin' Picnic was just the beginning. The new Associate Pastor is putting all kinds of ideas in Bill's mind about how to bring more people to church.

Nothing wrong with that – except that every new idea dumbs down the service a little more. We're supposed to replace classical music with "praise choruses." We're supposed to set up a projector so that a bouncing ball will spoon-feed the words of the praise choruses in real time to the congregation. And we're supposed to call the sanctuary a "worship center" – we're told this will appeal to people's modern consumer orientation.

None of these by itself would be so bad. Well, maybe the praise choruses. It's hard to see how that's a step up from the Fauré "Requiem," especially with that image of the pig with the apple in its mouth still fresh in my mind.

But it's not any one thing – it's the overall direction. They want to remove anything they think is a barrier, but they're removing the substance right along with it. As things are going, we'll get more and more people to come and be entertained – kind of like going to the movies.

I've been fighting this for a while. Each of my protests has fallen on deaf ears or been patiently countered with a "you need to understand where people are coming from today." Finally, I told Bill, "All you're worried about is getting new people in the door at any price. You're going to spend all your energy on the new people who are drawn to the entertainment, not the content. And then you're going to start losing your foundational members, the ones who volunteer, run programs, and yes, give money."

But this still-green-behind-the-ears pastor has convinced Bill otherwise. Everything has to change to draw people in – from the terminology to the layout of the service and even to the parking lot (one of Bill's main goals *now is to build a bigger parking lot because if people have a hard time finding a space this Sunday, they might not return next Sunday).*

And it's hitting me where I live – the music. I already try to do a variety of music to make everyone happy. But now, classical music is supposed to be kept to a minimum, lest it discourage someone from attending church. The great works of Bach, which have stirred the religious imagination of Christians for hundreds of years. The near-perfection of Mozart's "Requiem." Handel's "Messiah." Brahms. Beethoven. All reduced to nothing more than an impediment.

Christianity has a treasure of some of the greatest music ever written, by the greatest musicians in history, and composed, as Bach said of his own music, "for the glory of God." I'm now told this is not enough to move people. We need to replace it with music that was composed today and will be gone tomorrow and whose every note screams "mediocrity!"

To make a long and frustrating story short, this is not what I signed up for. I submitted my resignation today. It is probably one of the best things I ever did.

Right after I resigned, I called Evelyn Troxler, who runs the Opera in the Schools program. She asked me to come over right away and audition. And they want me to play the leading role!

Ok, so it's a children's opera called "Sid the Serpent Who Wanted to Sing." I'm going to play a snake in hundreds of schools throughout Texas next year. Not quite the Metropolitan Opera. But it will be a relief to leave behind my sixty-plus hours a week at the church, and just focus on performing and continuing to teach at St. Mary's University.

And besides, I've never played a serpent before. Once we start rehearsals, I don't think I'm going to miss the church work. Shortly after you and I met, we had begun to talk about going back to school once you finish your Air Force enlistment, and I think we ought to give it serious thought. But in the meantime, it's going to be a great year, slithering through the schools of Texas.

Love,

Gayle

৵৹

August 2, 1990

Dear Gayle,

Sid the Serpent Who Wanted to Sing – it has a nice ring to it. Instead of trying to squeeze your music into the church's dumbed down approach, you'll be showing thousands of schoolchildren that good music can also be fun. And surely a singing snake is better than a roasted pig.

On one of my first visits to Colonial Hills Church, the Associate Pastor told me that the average person in South Texas listens to country music on the way to the mall and the movies. So he needs to have the same experience at church or he won't relate to it. I think the opposite is true. If Colonial Hills tries to compete with Disney, why go? People can drive right by the church and on to the mall, with Kenny Rogers blaring through the speakers. Colonial Hills will do better offering what people aren't already getting, and what only they can offer.

I fear that people at the church will think I am the real reason you left, no matter what you say. It's selfish of me to feel this way. You're doing this for your own happiness. But I wonder if people at Colonial Hills will think, "She married a Jew, and here she is leaving the church a couple of months later." Maybe I should go back to what I've said before, and not worry what people say or think about our marriage.

Love,

Harold

&

September 8, 1990

Dear Gayle,

I've been assaulted. Sam is his name. He is a saxophonist in the Air Force Band. No, I wasn't hit over the head with a saxophone – only a Bible.

We are sitting in the belly of a C-5 Air Force plane, cruising at 35,000 feet, on our way to the Azores Archipelago. Located almost 1,000 miles off the coast of Portugal, the Azores comprise nine islands dotted with picture postcard fishing villages. I've yet to discern what possessed the Air Force to catapult an entire band here. But it's a welcome diversion from our usual bus tours through rural Texas.

The C-5 is the largest cargo plane in the world, six stories high and nearly the length of a football field. The band members sit ensconced in one little corner of the plane. We're really just part of the cargo, trying not to move around too much in our crude web seating as the plane lurches through air turbulence. I'm holding on tight. Sam is in the seat next to me. There's nowhere to go until the plane touches down, which is still several hours off.

Sam is an evangelical Christian. He's a nice guy with a strong faith. Maybe a little too strong. He learned that I am Jewish, and although we get along well on a personal level, I seem to have become a project of his. We've had a few conversations before. But with no escape route available, this conversation goes on and on.

Sam gives me a full overview of his faith and what he is sure is missing from my own. He takes out a Bible and runs through a litany of passages to prove his points. But after a couple of hours of conversation, his assertions about salvation being possible only through Jesus, his enumeration of the rabbis' "mistakes" in interpreting the Christian message, and his absolute certainty that he is right are beginning to wear on me.

The problem is that with my Reform Hebrew School education, I am left in the dust. This passage "proves" that Jesus was born of a virgin; that passage is irrefutable evidence that only Jesus can be the suffering servant (whatever that is!); yet another passage is an invitation to worship Jesus as God's son. This may all be second nature to experienced Christians, but it's hardly the stuff on which I was raised.

Many a Jew may not be as familiar with these passages as are Christians. If a Christian's very belief system rises or falls on a set of verses proving something about Jesus, then the verses must be front and center. They don't occupy the same place in Judaism, and so Jews don't spend the same time memorizing them.

If that were the only issue in our lopsided conversation, then I wouldn't give it much thought. I could simply cut Sam off with the stock Jewish response –"I respect your beliefs, and am not trying to convert you. I ask that you give me the same respect."

But something here runs much deeper, and keeps gnawing at me. It's not simply that I'm less familiar with these passages. I've never seen them before. I feel like a complete ignoramus about my own Bible. Muslims were the first to call Jews the "People of the Book." No one in all my years of Hebrew School thought to tell me a whole lot about this Book which supposedly has people like me as its subject.

The Azores are beautiful. But I'm distracted. My conversation with Sam replays in my mind even as we perform back-to-back performances across the islands. Sam implies that the rabbis are hiding things from me because they don't want me to know the truth. I find it hard to believe that at some point over the past 2,000 years, no rabbi thought to look at these passages. No rabbi interpreted these passages differently. No rabbi understood the Christian interpretation yet still believed it to be incorrect. If it were as simple as Sam tries to make it, then Jews would have been shown these passages long ago, immediately realized the error of their ways, and converted.

That has not happened, so obviously I am missing something. Actually, I suspect that I am missing a lot.

In practical terms, this means that I am seeing these passages for the first time through Sam's missionizing eyes. If the suffering servant passage of Isaiah is not speaking about Jesus, then I don't know what the other options are. If the Bible isn't really speaking about a virgin birth, then I don't know about what it is speaking.

Sam's conclusions about these passages all seem reasonable enough on the surface. But there must be another side, or the rabbis would all be ministers by now.

I need to do some research. As soon as we touch down again in San Antonio, I'm going to speak with Rabbi Schwartzman.

Love,

Harold

࿔

November 14, 1990

Dear Gayle,

I knew there had to be more to this story. I showed Rabbi Schwartzman all of Sam's passages, and he went through them with me. For some of the passages, the verses surrounding them provide the context and essentially negate the meaning that Sam has ascribed to them. For others, the original Hebrew yields meanings that are rather different from the English translations that Sam is using. Unfortunately, beyond recognizing the letters of the Hebrew alphabet and words like "good" and "thank you," I have no way of understanding the Hebrew. Then again, neither does Sam. I wish, though, that I knew enough to be able to read this in the original and figure it out for myself.

I went back to Sam, ready to do battle with my new knowledge. I had no idea he would side-step me and simply choose different weapons. He looked surprised when I challenged him, acting as if I had actually studied these passages and knew something about them. Sam usually has a big smile on his face. This time, the smile faded, and I thought I caught a flicker of doubt sweeping across his eyes.

A few days later, he came back, smile intact. No doubt, he had spoken with his own resident expert. He made a few comments about the passages we had discussed, although it seemed like a weak rebuttal if you ask me.

Just as I was beginning to think I was out of the woods, he trotted out new passages. I was prepared only to discuss the initial verses. Some nerve, just when I'm scoring points, to deflect and cite other passages that I've never seen. To make matters worse, Sam put a book in my hands by a so-called "Messianic Jew," supposedly a scholar. Not surprisingly, the book claims that Jesus was the messiah and the Jews are wrong.

Of course, I did the prudent thing. I retreated gracefully, and then met again with Rabbi Schwartzman. As with the previous meeting, the rabbi took me through the verses and showed me that Sam's presentation left something to be desired. I showed him the book, and he pointed out several errors as he glanced through it.

Then, he surprised me. "Where," he asked, "is all of this leading? You'll keep coming to me. He'll keep going to his pastor. And we'll have a disputation by proxy. What's the point?"

I mumbled something about not having a lot of knowledge and just needing to understand this well enough so I could fend off attempts to convert me. "So go get the knowledge. But get the knowledge about Judaism, not just about why you aren't a Christian."

He has a point. I should be able to go through that Messianic book and recognize its false claims. But even if I could do that, I would only have articulated why I am not a Christian (or at least not an Evangelical one). There are billions of people in the world who are not Christian. That still doesn't define me as a Jew.

Here in South Texas, several people who have never before met a Jew in their lives have asked me what Jews believe. I've told them that Jews basically believe what Christians do, except for the part about Jesus. But all I have been saying is that Jews don't believe in Jesus. I have been defining Judaism by what it is not. I can't give a coherent description of what Judaism is. That, I'm afraid, would take much more knowledge than I possess.

This revelation of mine fits squarely within one of Sam's arguments. Beyond truncated and questionably translated verses, Sam has been saying that Jews are not receptive to Jesus' message because of 2,000 years of anti-Semitism. The book he gave me makes the same point. The point is insulting in a way, because it implies that if only Jews could look past the persecution to the truth of the religious claims, then they would understand their error and see the light. In other words, the Jews' objections to Jesus are purely emotional and lack any theological legitimacy. All that is left to discuss is whether Christians can be nice to Jews, and Jews can now move on and get over it.

As much as Sam's argument repels me, I know many Jews who think that way, who define themselves by anti-Semitism. Being Jewish becomes a way of speaking out against people who hate you.

I must admit that I've succumbed to this mindset more than a few times. But if I only define myself by what others think of me, then I haven't defined myself at all. If people hate the Jews, then that defines them, not the Jews. It is a bit disturbing to have come into adulthood thinking I had a strong Jewish identity, only to realize that I can't define who I am from the inside. It seems daunting, but I need to find my way to an answer. When or how, I don't know.

There is yet another nagging feeling that this encounter has spawned. Your position is not entirely clear to me. When we began dating, you said that you needed to be a Christian, but that you saw that I had a relationship with God and accepted that I had no need for Jesus. My encounter with Sam leaves me feeling like I need more of a relationship with God beyond simply "not with Jesus."

It leaves me with something else. I have just spent the past couple of months tearing apart many of the Biblical verses on which Christian theology is based. I did this first as a matter of religious self-defense, and then as a matter of intellectual curiosity. But at the end of this lengthy exercise, I walk away certain that those verses don't mean what many Christians say they do.

By rejecting Christianity, I mean no disrespect. I can appreciate how much Sam's faith means to him. However, I would also unequivocally say that Jesus is neither the messiah nor the son of God. For a Christian who does believe these things, and whose very life is based on them, my disagreement could be taken as intolerance. But unlike a missionary, I am not trying to persuade anyone to give up their religion.

I respect your Christian faith. However, by definition, my viewpoint as a Jew, accepting as I might be, still defines your beliefs as incorrect – at least on some level. In turn, your belief in Jesus is at odds with my own beliefs. We've existed quite happily with this dichotomy, and I'm not suggesting it need be an issue. I'm just curious how you resolve it in your own mind, or whether you even think there is anything to resolve. Perhaps our common ground renders our theological differences inconsequential. That is, until you are cornered by a saxophonist.

Love,

Harold

∂∽∽

November 16, 1990

Dear Harold,

Much of what we believe comes from the families into which we were born. You were born into a family which, as far as we know, has always been Jewish. I was born into a family which, as far as we know, has always been Christian. Many families have always been Buddhist, Moslem, Hindu, and so on. Each one thinks that their way is the one true way. But then, they can't all be correct. Do you think everyone else in the world is wrong? So we have to conclude that for each family, their way is the only or at least best way for them.

It's not this simple, though, because being born into Judaism isn't the same as being born into Christianity or some other religions. Christianity is solely a faith, not an ethnicity. Judaism is both. Christians who want to convert Jews often feel conflicted about what it is they are trying to change. They convince themselves that it can't be because of ethnicity, because that would make them racists. So the need to change the faith takes on monumental importance.

How hard do you think Sam would work on you if you were Muslim or Hindu? He knows he could much more easily convert someone if it were only a matter of their belief system. But he can't change your identity as a Jew, which underneath the surface is very frustrating for him.

That's why some Christians say "completed Jew" rather than "converted Jew." It allows them to tell a Jew that he can keep his identity even if he gives up his beliefs. That's also why people like Sam hold out

Messianic Judaism as the perfect solution. But that's not what the Bible actually says. The Bible says that God chose the Israelites to be a people who would live in certain ways that were not expected of everyone else. I don't understand why someone who isn't Jewish feels the need to take a Jew away from that.

True, I think some of those laws are antiquated. But not all. I love celebrating Hanukkah and the Passover Seders with you, and Rosh Hashanah and Yom Kippur have become very meaningful for me. But the idea of a "Chosen People" is at the same time curious, inspirational, and terribly frustrating. Why do you get to be the one who is chosen? Does this mean that I'm not chosen? Do you ever wish you weren't chosen? Do you look down on those of us who aren't? Can people become chosen? Can people choose not to be chosen?

I haven't fully responded to your original concern – how can we both be right? I was raised to believe that if you weren't a Christian, you weren't going to heaven: no Jesus – no salvation. Growing up, I remember a sermon Reverend Ranney preached about the Trinity. He said all of the Trinity represents God. The Father, Son, and Holy Ghost are all the same Being, but Christians relate to each of the three in a different way. Reverend Ranney is one person, but his parents see him as a child, his wife as a husband, and his children as a father. All my life, I have believed that God was in the form of this Trinity – God, Holy Spirit and Jesus – and all three ways of relating to God were necessary.

When I've spent so much of my life believing this, it's hard all of a sudden to believe that someone else's relationship with God can be so direct as not to need the Trinity and not to need Jesus. But I realized very quickly after I met you that that is your reality.

When the Israelites were in the desert, Moses was not permitted to see God's face, lest the power overwhelm him. Maybe Christians relate to God somewhat in this way, praying through Jesus and focusing on the Trinity so as not to be overwhelmed by direct, unmediated communication.

As I write this, I start wondering if only certain people can have this direct relationship, or if someone can communicate with God in this way without being a member of the Chosen People. I don't have the answers, but regarding your initial question, I think both of us can be right for ourselves. For you, Judaism can be complete. For me, Judaism would not be complete because I was born a Gentile. Jews received the Ten Commandments di-

rectly from God at Mount Sinai. Gentiles didn't. We need another way to receive what God wants to give us.

At least that's what I've come to believe observing you and your family, and people of other religions.

Love,

Gayle

⨯⨯

November 19, 1990

Dear Gayle,

Perhaps, as you say, Jews are supposed to connect differently to God because that's what the Torah says. But it seems to me that it's easier for a Jew to say that his way is right for him but not for others than it would be for a Christian. Sam's point is that either Jesus is the Messiah for everyone, or for no one.

Even if I don't personally believe that Jesus was the Messiah, much less the son of God, I can still respect those who do. I can admire their faith, the comfort that it brings them, and the positive impact it has on their lives. But for the Christian, it seems there would be some cognitive dissonance to say that Jesus is the Messiah, the only begotten son of God who rose from the dead, but that he need not be the Messiah for everyone.

I've met liberal Christians who do believe exactly that. Perhaps they simply value their relationships with people of other faiths more than theological exactitude. Or perhaps, like you, they see a relationship with God in other people, and cannot abandon what their own eyes tell them in favor of abstract concepts that may conflict. That's basically what you've been telling me since you met me – that you see that I have a relationship with God – although I must admit it's not something I see in myself so readily.

So in the end, nothing has really changed. We've existed quite nicely with our different beliefs, and my conversations with

Sam haven't changed at all how we relate to one another. But what I've taken away from this is that I need to understand better what Judaism is and what it means to me. Rabbi Schwartzman did recommend another temple when I complained about our experience at Beth El. They're Reconstructionist – I think it's like Reform, but I'm not sure. They are a small group called Beth Am, who meet at the Jewish Community Center, and they discuss the Torah as part of the service. Maybe it'll be a start.

Love,

Harold

&

January 26, 1991

Dear Harold,

As I fumbled through the pages of the prayer book, I wondered if someone in San Antonio offers a crash course in Hebrew. Every time they said a prayer in English, I breathed a sigh of relief. But the English was much harder to come by than at the Reform service. I initially felt disappointed to walk into the bare side room at the Jewish Community Center and see only 25 people. It's an adjustment from the overflow crowds I've grown used to on Sunday mornings. But the small size in the small space lent an intimacy that was refreshing. I learned they call a group like this a "chavurah," but no one told me what the word means.

I was just beginning to feel comfortable when they called you up front, leaving me with the mostly Hebrew prayer book and no instruction manual. An all-out panic attack ensued when they asked me to carry the Torah around the congregation. I wasn't sure if this was kosher, but I knew everything would be ok when you leaned over and whispered, "You know what to do, don't you?" And I did – I just thought back to what I saw on Yom Kippur and did the same thing.

Still, it was quite a sight – a Christian parading a Torah around with Jews touching their prayer shawls to it.

The most moving part came at the end, during the baby naming when the grandmother rose to speak. I couldn't stop staring at the tears in her eyes and the numbers on her arm, as she told us about the dark time when she never dared to dream she would survive, much less in her wildest imagination see herself standing here in the United States as her granddaughter was dedicated to God.

Despite the Hebrew, the feeling at this chavurah (whatever that is) is much more comfortable than the cold snobbery I felt at Beth El. Perhaps Beth El was too cavernous with too few people. Or the congregation didn't have any spirit. Or the people seemed like they were there to fulfill some kind of obligation and get home. Whatever it was, I didn't feel welcome.

Something about the rabbi's sermon that night at Beth El made me feel even less welcome. I can't put my finger on it, maybe that he seemed self-absorbed. Or maybe it was the unspoken message that shouted, "Jews don't do anything wrong. They are only wronged by the world." I know Jews have a long history of persecution, but the congregants will learn and grow more from serious introspection than from hearing how downtrodden they are. I feel the same way when a minister doesn't challenge the congregation.

These thoughts came to me during the Torah discussion at Beth Am. This is the first time I've seen Jews grappling with their own Bible. People unhesitatingly aired their differing views, arguing, sometimes almost shouting at one another. And it was wonderful, because they acted like it mattered.

And in contrast to Beth El, Julie Danan, the prayer leader, came over and introduced herself after the service. She's impressive. Through all the back and forth of the Torah discussion, she always seemed able to relate what people said to something from Scripture and show how it relates to our lives. Although the organ and professional quartet of Beth El is more familiar territory for me, it seems like Beth Am is the right place if we're going to go to Jewish services.

Love,

Gayle

ॐ♥ॐ

March 3, 1991

Dear Gayle,

Friday night at the Danans was full of surprises. The first
surprise was that they invited us, and only a few weeks after we
began going to services. The Danans seem so traditional, not the
type who would want to bring an interfaith family into their home.
I assume Julie knows our situation. It's obvious, at least, that we
don't know as much about Judaism as they do and don't observe all
the things that they do.

I was nervous about going, since neither of us knows much
about what observant Jews do on Friday night. I feared we might
embarrass ourselves out of ignorance, but Julie genuinely wanted
us to come.

Even though they were very nice to us, and they have such a
warm relationship with their four children, the whole evening felt
awkward. Maybe it's because I've never been to a traditional Friday
night dinner before. There were times I felt like I didn't know what
was going on, and was missing important cues.

The awkwardness began upon our arrival. Julie did tell us to
be at their apartment by 6:15 for candle lighting. I didn't think it
would matter that we arrived at 6:30, since our errands took longer
than expected. No big deal – we've been late to dinner at people's
homes before.

So I was surprised to see a set of lit Shabbat candles perched on
the dining room breakfront. I don't understand why they couldn't have
waited. Julie said something about needing to light the candles before
sunset. I've certainly never done it that way. In fact, on Friday nights at
the Monroe Temple of Liberal Judaism, I remember that they always
lit Shabbat candles after the 8:30 service had started, long after dark. I
don't understand why the sun's setting should override including your
guests in the candle lighting that they invited you to in the first place.
They didn't seem upset by it, but I still had the feeling that we had
messed up. And after all, we were only fifteen minutes late.

My awkwardness grew to embarrassment with the CD incident. I had found that beautiful CD of the Moscow Synagogue

Choir last month at the Tower Records in Austin. I brought it specifically because the Choir sings Shabbat songs, and I thought it would add to the atmosphere while we ate dinner. My only intention was to contribute something that would enrich the evening. How was I to know that they don't use electronics on Shabbat?

Julie wouldn't even let me put the CD in myself when I offered, even though the CD player was sitting right there next to the Shabbat candles. I don't understand why this is such an issue for them. If they must light candles at a certain time and not a minute later, and they can't even listen to a CD or watch TV, I wonder how they have any fun on Shabbat. It's all a bit fanatical. And yet they seem like such clear-headed, intelligent people.

Just as I began to feel more relaxed during the meal, they started singing all of those Hebrew songs, which are almost as much of a mystery to me as they are to you. It's a little embarrassing when the eight year old girl sitting next to you knows these songs cold, and you're sitting there with a smile on your face, hoping no one will notice that you're not singing. That they were singing in multiple keys and off-key didn't help. The CD would have sounded much better.

The evening pulled me in two directions. A mysterious feeling of warmth pervaded the dinner table. Yet, I felt ill at ease. It wasn't just the timing of the candle lighting, or the CD faux pas, or even not having a clue about the songs they sang. It's that I don't fully get what they are doing. I don't understand why everything has to be so strict. I don't know how to make sense of their world. Pieces of it are attractive. But I still am standing on the outside looking in.

If one Shabbat meal engendered all of these feelings in me, then I'm curious to know what it did for you. And that brings me to the biggest surprise of the evening. I want to make sure I heard correctly what you said when we went to the supermarket after leaving the Danans.

"I just don't think I could ever convert because of the music. I need a good musical experience."

That was what I heard you say, framed by silence on my part. I admit that I too am struggling to find satisfaction with the folk music tradition common to most synagogues when I am used to the world of Beethoven and Mozart. However, my great musical experiences always have been in secular settings, so it doesn't bother me in the same way that it obviously bothers you.

Musical dissatisfaction aside, I had no idea that converting had ever entered into your thoughts. It hadn't entered into mine, and in all of our discussions, it's never come up. I'm not suggesting that it should. I'm surprised, that's all. You started fasting on Yom Kippur a few months after I met you. Not exactly a joyful introduction to Judaism, but one you chose to do all on your own. And you were the one who suggested we light Shabbat candles, at whatever time we might choose to light them. Now, not in response to anyone's inquiry, you are explaining why you couldn't convert. Yet until a few months ago, you were working full-time in a church. I need to understand what you're thinking.

Love,

Harold

৵৽

May 19, 1991

Dear Harold,

I closed the book on Beth El a little too soon.

There's a Jewish holiday, I don't know what you call it, but it celebrates Jews receiving the Torah at Mount Sinai. Anyway, this year it was on a Sunday, which conflicted with the temple organist's church job. Knowing that I had left Colonial Hills Church, she thought to call me.

This must be a minor holiday, because they held it in the small chapel for the handful of people who showed up. The chapel is equipped with a beautiful portative pipe organ. But had I not had the tenor soloist guiding me, I would have had no idea when in the service to play it. It's a different service than they do at Beth Am – and it's certainly different from what I did at Colonial Hills.

The rabbi spoke about the Jews receiving the Ten Commandments. The way he discussed the Biblical text was different from how most ministers do it. He spoke at length about what the words mean in the original Hebrew, something ministers rarely do. I've heard sermons about the Ten Commandments many times, but never like this.

A pity more people didn't come. Even with the rabbi, it's hard to be inspired when the other congregants don't seem to be. All in all, I still prefer Beth Am.

Love,

Gayle

❧❧

July 17, 1991

Dear Gayle,

Lots of changes from just a year ago – we get married, you trade in your church robe for a serpent costume – and next month, we'll experience the joys of driving a U-Haul 2,000 miles to Boston. I think I have the bigger adjustment. Doctoral studies in music connect with everything you've done before, whereas law school is a different planet from the Air Force Band.

The Band was nice for four years, but it convinced me I don't want to make a career of it.

I have no desire to watch the Rio Grande Valley again through a bus window for hundreds of miles en route to the next concert. I won't get upset if I never again perform in a high school auditorium located this side of nowhere and then eat at the Dairy Queen because it's the only restaurant in town. And I don't feel the need to play "Stars and Stripes Forever" one more time – the first 500 repetitions left it permanently engraved on my brain.

Playing in the Air Force Band sometimes feels like the musical equivalent of being a short order cook. I need to regain that sense of magic I discovered the first time I played. And I can best do that by playing music on my own terms while doing something else for a livelihood.

I don't know what to expect out of law school, other than that I'll have to work hard. I like the idea of studying law, but I'm not sure I want to be a lawyer. People have told me, though, that many law school graduates wind up doing other things. Whatever happens, we'll be in Boston, where I'm pretty sure there are no Dairy Queens.

Love,

Harold

ॐ◌ॐ

August 28, 1991

Dear Harold,

I thought we'd never make it to the East Coast. Bad enough that we had to pack the truck ourselves in the 100 degree San Antonio summer heat. Then we had to drive the thing through state after state. Tennessee is particularly long – of course it gets much longer when the U-Haul breaks down twice, once at each end of the state.

When the first U-Haul technician came out and had to fix the gears, I should have known we weren't going to make it to Boston in that truck. There was no room for doubt, however, when a distinct burning smell wafted from the gear box, and then the truck would only go into reverse regardless of what gear it was in.

The only good thing about the experience was that, arriving in Knoxville with the broken truck at 2 a.m. and nowhere to go, we got to spend the night with the Freestates, whom I had known from Colonial Hills Church when they lived in San Antonio. Robbie is one of those gentle ministers for whom the pulpit isn't a fit. And Irma and I have a special bond, since we together wrote our own musical, Mary, Servant of God, *for the Colonial Hills youth choir. It's quite a moving show, and* since Irma had me in mind for the role of Mary, maybe I'll get to perform it someday.

It was a welcome relief that my parents traveled with us the rest of the way, and your parents too once we got to New York. My father enjoyed seeing the signs in Connecticut for Farmington, presumably where the town of my childhood got its name.

When my mom pulled out the ham sandwiches for lunch, I realized I hadn't told her that you've decided not to eat pork. Fortunately, she also had a tuna sandwich so you didn't have to choose between ham and starvation. You said you decided to cut pork from your diet "to do something." I don't understand what you meant by that, but I have no problem with it since I never liked ham anyway.

If our parents hadn't bonded with each other before, the Boston experience took care of that. In addition to what I learned about moving, I also learned never to rent a place sight unseen. That a baby grand piano came with the house enticed me. That upon our arrival, the place looked like it hadn't been cleaned since it was built didn't thrill me as much. The six of us cleaning side by side for three days was a sight to behold.

Anyone watching our parents together would have been amazed how two Jews from metropolitan New York and two Christians from Central Illinois farm country get along so well. Hour after hour of power cleaning would have frayed anyone's nerves, and yet our parents seemed to enjoy being together through all the dirt and grime. We're really lucky.

Boston College Law School and the Boston University Doctoral program both start in just a week. So now it's time to hit the books and find jobs. And now that we're settled in New England, I've learned two things from this experience – I don't want to be a professional mover, and I never want to see a U-Haul again.

Love,

Gayle

∂∾≼

September 19, 1991

Dear Gayle,

I've been reading about Franz Rosenzweig, and I thought about him as I sat through the Kol Nidre service at that Reform temple in Newton. I concluded that had he lived today, he might well be one of the world's great Christian theologians. Rosenzweig came to adulthood at the turn of the 20th century, and is recorded by history as one of Judaism's greatest theologians of modern times. He got there by an unusual route, one that might not work for him today.

Rosenzweig lived in Germany at a time when assimilation was the norm. Many Jews with little or no Jewish background were converting to Christianity, as much out of a need to identify with the larger society to which they had assimilated, as out of genuine religious conviction. Heinrich Heine, the great German poet, called his conversion from Judaism to Christianity "the ticket of admission into European culture."

At the urging of a cousin who already had converted, the young Rosenzweig decided to become a Christian. Before doing so, he passed by a synagogue in Berlin on Yom Kippur. Upon hearing Kol Nidre and witnessing the intensity of the people around him asking God's forgiveness, he was overcome by what some have called a mystical experience. From the Berlin synagogue, he never made it to the baptismal font. As Rosenzweig wrote to a friend a few days later, "After prolonged, and I believe thorough, self-examination, I have reversed my decision. It no longer seems necessary to me, and therefore being what I am, no longer possible. I shall remain a Jew."

I'm envisioning a young Franz Rosenzweig today. On his way to the church on Yom Kippur Eve, he passes a synagogue like the one we went to, and something about the place beckons. He walks up the steps, thinking he perhaps should give Judaism a try before leaving it.

"Tickets, tickets. Do you have your tickets?" Rosenzweig looks up, shaken from the debate that had been raging in his mind.

Before him is a table full of envelopes. Presiding over the table is the man who half shouted at him.

"You need a ticket to get in. What's your name?" "Franz Rosenzweig," Rosenzweig mumbles, not quite sure what this has to do with his existential religious issue.

"Let's see," says the ticket maven. "Rose, Rosen, Rosenberg, Rosenthal. No Rosenzweig here. Would you have reserved them under a different name? What? You didn't buy tickets? Are you a student? We have a special deal for students, but you were supposed to have signed up in advance. Wait right here. I need to speak with the Chair of our ticket committee to see if we can make any accommodation."

Assuming Rosenzweig made it past the gatekeeper, he would then enter the sanctuary, knowing he had arrived in this place because he was searching for something, and hoping there was life beyond the ticket table.

Once inside, he might happen to sit among people like those in the Berlin synagogue. Or more likely, he would take in the beautiful prayers on this holiest night of the Jewish calendar, simultaneously hearing all around him the kind of conversation that I heard:

"Our Father, our King, hear our prayer. Our Father, our King, we have sinned before you."

"Gladys, what a beautiful dress. It's even nicer than what you wore last year for High Holidays. Did you lose weight? It looks so good on you. Where did you get it?"

"The Merciful One who answers the poor, may He answer us. The Merciful One Who answers the brokenhearted, may He answer us. The Merciful One Who answers the humble of spirit, may He answer us."

"Can you believe what that idiot did? What a pathetic excuse for a governor – he doesn't understand a thing about the economy."

"On Rosh Hashanah will be inscribed and on Yom Kippur will be sealed how many will pass from the earth and how many will be created; who will live and who will die . . . who will rest and who will wander, who will live in harmony and who will be harried, who will enjoy tranquility and who will suffer, who will be impoverished and who will be enriched, who will be degraded and who will be exalted."

"These services are SO long. I don't know why I come back every year. It better be over in time for me to get home and watch the ball game."

As the doors would open, out would walk Franz Rosenzweig, never to return, destined to become one of the great Christian theologians of his day.

With temples like this, I wonder how many Franz Rosenzweigs Judaism loses every year.

Love,

Harold

ન્જ્જ

October 6, 1991

Dear Harold,

I don't know what Franz Rosenzweig would have done, but I do know that I have no desire to return. Beth Am it was not.

I have done my research, however, and am happy to recommend another synagogue for you to try. There is a group called the Newton Centre Minyan, just down the road from the law school. It sounds a lot like Beth Am – small, intimate, and a bit on the traditional side. They meet every Saturday morning.

You may be wondering how I've so quickly become a Massachusetts synagogue expert. My information has come from a most unlikely source.

When I began my job a few weeks ago as the soprano soloist for First Baptist Church in Newton, I happened to mention to the minister that you are Jewish. Tom is very active in the Newton Interfaith Clergy Association, and is good friends with some of the rabbis.

But the Newton Center Minyan doesn't have a rabbi. Nor do they have a space of their own. They meet in a spare room of the church. That's how Tom knows so much about them.

So there is now a Baptist minister who is recommending that you go to synagogue.

Love,

Gayle

৵৶

January 11, 1992

Dear Gayle,

I escaped at the first opportunity. Forty-five minutes at the Newton Center Minyan was all I could handle before I turned tail and ran for cover.

Now I know why I put off going for months. I was nervous that I might feel out of place. And I did.

Beth Am was a leap – a lot more Hebrew than I had ever seen in my life. But there was English too, and the Torah discussions were always interesting. It was like going to high school with an elementary school education. A little tough, but I could manage. The Newton Center Minyan is like Jewish graduate school. Virtually all in Hebrew. No one to explain things to you. No one to tell you what page you're on, or aren't.

As the minutes dragged by, I felt like more and more eyes were focusing on me. They were wondering who is this new person who doesn't seem to have a clue what's going on. Why is he on the wrong page? Why is he still on the wrong page? Why did he just sit down while the rest of us are still standing? Why isn't he singing along?

I tried to leave unnoticed, slowly reaching for my tallis bag, the one I still have from my Bar Mitzvah. As I opened it, our High Holiday tickets from the Reform temple leapt onto the floor. "Aha!," they must be thinking, "September was the last time he went to services." Which is true.

I retreated gracelessly, wondering how, after all those years of Hebrew school, trying to pray from a traditional prayer book feels like traveling to a foreign country. Then I thought about all of those eyes staring at me. Well, perhaps they weren't staring. Actually, no one said or did anything to make me feel uncomfortable. I felt uncomfortable all on my own. That awkward feeling came from my own inability to follow the service. That voice of ridicule came, not from them, but from inside my own head.

As I dashed from the room into the First Baptist Church hallway, I thought about how much easier it is for me to follow a church service than a traditional Jewish one. True, the church service is never more than an hour, has a simple structure, and most important, is entirely in English. But Judaism is supposed to be my religion. It would be nice at least to be able to follow the service. But I'm not even sure where to start.

Love,

Harold

స్తిఌ

April 13, 1992

Dear Gayle,

I'm ready for the Seder. Matzah – check. Manischewitz wine – check. Maxwell House Hagaddahs – check.

I've been meaning to ask about the second night of Passover. Would you consider the possibility of a small Seder at our place? Since we need to leave my parents' house in the morning to get back to Boston anyway, we have the second night free. And no Seder invitation.

Meanwhile, two of my law school classmates aren't going home and have nowhere to go. Their Jewish background is like mine, so they're not expecting something elaborate. They just like the idea of having a Seder. We can do anything we want with good old Maxwell House. And they're students – any food we serve them will be a step up from what they usually eat.

Love,

Harold

⊱⊰

April 18, 1992

Dear Harold,

Congratulate me – I now hold the honor of successfully hosting my first Passover Seder! When you asked, my mind saw images of women frantically cleaning the house, assembling the items for the Seder plate, getting the Seder table ready, and at the same time preparing a lavish meal delivered piping hot at the precise moment it is (finally) to be eaten.

Your mother helped to reassure me, and she even gave me a shank bone and roasted egg for our Boston Seder plate. And by following the Seder plate diagram in the Maxwell House Haggadah, along with the other instructions, we almost looked like we knew what we were doing.

A practiced Seder-goer might have turned up his nose, but Steve's and David's beaming expressions shouted, "I've missed this." At pivotal moments, one or the other would smile and say, "Oh, I remember this from when I was a kid." When we got to Dayeinu, I didn't think they'd ever stop laughing and singing. By the time we ended with "Next year in Jerusalem," they were already talking about doing this again next Passover.

For all the good feeling, something about the evening felt, well, I'm not sure – me, the Christian, helping reintroduce Jews to their own Passover Seder. I thought back to my days as an Evangelical bringing "lost souls" back to the fold. Except this is not my fold, and I first opened a Haggadah two years ago. Yet here I was, the "Evangelical," guiding Jews through a Seder, and helping to bring back long-dormant memories of childhood (which no doubt, included the same Maxwell House Hagaddah).

Even so, as we sat in our interfaith kitchen, now the staging ground for a Jewish celebration, their smiles made me smile. As I witnessed their initial near-apathy grow into excitement, I secretly hoped this evening would light a spark in them to bring more Judaism into their lives.

So much about Judaism is fun, and also meaningful. I'm puzzled why many Jews don't become more involved. Do you think this might be the start of a tradition for us?

Next year in – wherever we are!

Love,

Gayle

ᏸᎾᏸ

August 17, 1992

"Music can name the unnameable and communicate the unknowable." Leonard Bernstein

Dear Gayle,

Night after night, I've been sitting at the piano, fitting music to text, and discovering strands of myself. I keep probing when and why this inner drive announced its need to write music about the Holocaust. I never desired to compose before, but this music seems almost a prop that transports me to a shadow world I can't quite define.

Survivors weren't hard to come by growing up in Monroe. One time, while selling M&Ms for my Cub Scout troop, I found myself standing in front of Mrs. Pillberg's door. She lived at the top of a hill lined with 1950s ranch houses. As I rattled on about all the Cub Scout activities her M&Ms purchase would support, I could not take my eyes off those numbers on her arm staring back at me. Mrs. Pillberg never noticed my staring, or at least she never let on that she did. After all those years, she may have grown accustomed to involuntary stares – although she couldn't have gotten used to the numbers.

Then there was the boy in my Hebrew school class whose father seemed old and sad. His numbers stared back at us too, when for two hours he spoke of the nightmare those numbers had witnessed. And even our rabbi had come to the U.S. from Germany, passing through Buchenwald on the way.

Perhaps I'm composing because I'm trying to take this shadow world that lapped at the edges of my childhood, and make it real for myself. Not to my intellect, which requires no convincing. But to my heart, which can have its doubts. Whether confronted by the enormity of six million or the numbers on one arm, it is often too burdensome to acknowledge that this cataclysm is part of the human experience. One can get on in the world by ignoring reality, or by coming to terms with it. But how do you come to terms with the unshakeable evidence that, whatever humanity's capacity for good, it has an almost infinite capacity for evil?

Music is its own shadow world. It speaks beyond where my thoughts can take me. As the survivors' words meld into my own music, I am finding that place in myself for what I cannot articulate.

Sheltered by my American childhood, this musical exploration of mine is the closest I can come to understanding the survivors. The faded building across the park from where I now sit at the piano constantly reminds me of this gap. One needs a little imagination to see the long-abandoned edifice with the hole in its roof and the un-mown yard as Congregation Mishkan Tefila, where Leonard Bernstein celebrated his Bar Mitzvah.

At precisely the time when Mrs. Pillberg and the rest were hanging onto the precipice that was Nazi Germany, Leonard Bernstein was showing the world that a Jew in America could reach the very top. In 1939, just months after Kristallnacht, Bernstein made his first television appearance. In 1940, the year the Nazis chose the site for Auschwitz, Bernstein was studying conducting at Tanglewood with the great Serge Koussevitsky. In 1941, the Nazis set up Theresienstadt, and Bernstein conducted the Boston Pops. In 1943, the Nazis put down the Warsaw Ghetto uprising. That year, Bernstein made his historic debut with the New York Philharmonic, overnight becoming America's pre-eminent conductor.

Bernstein penned many compositions on Jewish themes, but virtually none confront the Holocaust. Perhaps the wound was too fresh, too raw to apply the salve of music.

I've discovered several poems for my own music that are helping me to glimpse the shadow world that suddenly has become so important. Some, as expected, speak of survivors' loss of faith, or question God's justice, or recount horrific events. But I've stumbled upon another vantage point that is too often obscured by the tragedy of it all.

Amidst the wreckage, there are more than a few who tenaciously kept their faith in the face of evil, affirmed God in the face of ungodliness, even spiritually defied those who sought to destroy the last remnant of their spirit. I have discovered people who in the camps risked their lives to make Hannukah menorahs out of potatoes, because that was all they had to celebrate Judaism's victory of the weak over the strong. Or who fasted on Yom Kippur when every day brought starvation.

In the final song of my piece, I am going to use this poem, which was found scrawled on the walls of a cellar in Cologne, Germany, where Jews hid from the Nazis:

I believe in the sun when it is not shining.
I believe in love even when feeling it not.
I believe in God, even when He is silent.

I am hungering to read more from the people who incomprehensibly kept their faith. I need to find out how they did it, and why.

In the meantime, I'll keep composing, and hope for some inspiration.

Love,

Harold

❧❦

August 17, 1992

Dear Harold,

I don't know how I first learned about the Holocaust. I don't remember ever not knowing about it. When I was young, as almost a rite of passage, I read The Diary of Anne Frank. *Ever since, I've read anything I could find about the destruction of Europe's Jews. I could never fathom how anyone could see another person, never mind a whole group of people, as animals. The irony, of course, is that the more the Nazis treated the Jews as less than human, the more the Nazis dehumanized themselves.*

It's scary to contemplate how such an insane person could so easily become the leader of one of the world's most civilized nations, intent on wiping out Jews and anyone else who got in his way. His single-minded hatred of the Jews overrode everything. I even read that, as the Allies were closing in on Germany, he continued to transport Jews to the camps at the expense of getting supplies to his own troops. For Hitler, killing the Jews became literally more important than winning the war. To this day, everything about the Holocaust is unfathomable.

Growing up on the farm, if a dog killed a chicken, Dad said the dog would have to be "put down" because once the dog tasted the chicken's blood, there would be no stopping him from attacking every chicken in the coop. A crude analogy, perhaps. But then, perhaps not – Hitler was such a dog. The more blood he tasted, the more he attacked.

Even if one writes him off as a one-time lunatic, it doesn't explain how he won over the masses. Maybe some were simply "obeying orders" for fear of their own lives, or maybe Hitler had a flair for surrounding himself with people who, like himself, were wholly evil. Or maybe the evil lay dormant under the surface and it was Hitler who had a special ability to bring it out. We'll never know.

Your chronicle of the gap between Bernstein's world and the world of the Holocaust is particularly apt. By composing your piece across the park from Bernstein's synagogue, perhaps you are in some way bringing those two worlds together. That Jews can move mountains in one civilization even as they are being wiped out in another may offer hope that one day Jews can overcome the senseless hatred which has plagued them throughout the centuries, and live freely everywhere, treated like the very special human beings that they are.

I can't wait to sing your piece. I just know it's going to be incredible.

Love,

Gayle

ॐ◈

September 2, 1992

Dear Harold,

Singing jobs come from the most unlikely places. Paul, one of the pianists from Boston University, called the other day to ask if I wanted a "temple gig." He's a member of Ohabei Shalom, that stately, Romanesque temple in Brookline. I just returned from my audition with Robbie Solomon, their Cantor.

I was nervous I wouldn't be able to handle the Hebrew. It turns out that you don't need to know Hebrew to sing in the choir. Everything is written out phonetically in English.

Robbie came to Ohabei Shalom fairly recently. He's also one of the lead singers for a band called Safam, which I've been told is big in the world of Jewish music. I wanted him to know that, even though I'm not Jewish, Judaism isn't totally alien to me. So I made sure he knew you are Jewish.

Robbie hired me on the spot. That I'm not Jewish didn't seem to be an issue for him. Oh, and he said I could get a free ticket for you. Ohabei Shalom is Reform, so you'll be back in familiar territory. And it has to be better than that place last year.

Love,

Gayle

ॐ◈

October 7 (after Yom Kippur), 1992

Dear Harold,

Rabbi Emily ran up to the balcony at the end of Yom Kippur and gushed, "Never in all of Judaism has there been a more fabulous choir!" Really? We eight singers were stuffed behind a wall upstairs where we couldn't see the congregation and they couldn't see us. I guess our distance was supposed to create the effect of hearing voices from another realm. But it was more like voices from another building singing through badly placed microphones. And the pianist played her electric keyboard, which gave off a tacky, Tin Pan Alley sound as an antique pipe organ lay dormant just steps away.

Do you realize this is the first Yom Kippur I haven't fasted since we met? The other soprano did fast, and as a result sounded flat on everything. So I think I was right to have lunch and keep drinking water. Funny – she is in the process of converting, but none of the other singers are Jewish or even thinking about becoming Jewish. In fact, like me, most of the other singers have church gigs.

Frances, the bass, did consider converting once years ago, but the rabbi talked him out of it – such a difference from churches who will welcome anyone who even hints that they might, maybe, kind of, possibly be interested in converting.

The service, what I could hear of it anyway from over the wall, was a bit touchy-feely for my tastes. And we weren't the most "fabulous choir in all of Judaism" – at least, I sure hope not. But the singers are nice and supportive of one another. And you get in free, so I think I'll do it next year.

Love,

Gayle

⊛

October 23, 1992

Dear Gayle,

In San Antonio, I loved going to Beth Am every week, getting to know people, and taking my first steps in learning about the Torah. But then we moved, and I've yet to regain my footing.

So I thought I'd try Ohabei Shalom for Friday night services. But Friday night at Ohabei Shalom happens in the small chapel, where the Yom Kippur crowd of hundreds suddenly dwindles to thirty or so. Most of them qualify for Social Security. Rabbi Emily gave an interesting sermon, but it's not enough. The room felt as if all the air had been sucked out of it, and I walked out knowing I'd like to come back, but knowing that I wouldn't.

We're in Boston, not the boondocks– there must be some congregation somewhere that offers substance and a feeling of community, but isn't so traditional that I can't access it. But I've been to three places already. I'd like to keep looking. However, with the demands of law school, I have neither the time nor the energy.

Love,

Harold

ॐॐ

December 20, 1992

Dear Gayle,

The egos wafted through the room even more than the smell of eggnog. Richard Casilly was gracious to host a Christmas party for all of his voice students and their significant others. I had just forgotten what it's like to be in a room full of singers.

Hi, my name is (fill in the blank), and I'm a soprano/alto/tenor/bass (fill in the blank). I specialize in Italian opera/German art song/Renais-

sance women composers (fill in the blank). Let me tell you where I've sung recently, who loves my voice, and the amazingly fabulous career I have.

Omitted from the account is that they are spending more time waiting tables than singing.

Nor does the conversation ever venture beyond their glorious careers, because they don't care about anything except whether the world thinks they're God's gift to singing.

I know what a tough business it is. But is all the bluster really necessary? I've always thought of music as one of humanity's deepest forms of expression, not merely as a cover for a shaky sense of self.

Then again, not every singer is like that. You're not like that. With you, the music speaks for itself. Richard Casilly isn't like that – I suppose someone who's had a successful career at the Metropolitan Opera doesn't need to put up a front. Perhaps it's unavoidable for some to get swept up in the rush of ego when you have to invest so much of yourself in the music.

Oh, well. The eggnog was excellent.

Love,

Harold

&⚬⚭

April 20, 1993

Dear Harold,

I was right to leave Boston University – I agree, the egos are a bit much. Over at the Longy School of Music, I'm finding that people spend more time working on their craft than trying to convince you how wonderful they are. And making the switch helped me land a college teaching job for next year. One woman in the program teaches at Atlantic Union College in Lancaster, but she's moving this summer.

Atlantic Union College is a Seventh Day Adventist school. I've taught at religious colleges before, but this is uncharted territory. Since I'm ecumenical anyway, everything should be fine. The only rules that Marjo-rie, the Director of Music, gave me, are that I can't take any of the students out for lunch and order alcoholic drinks. I think I'll manage not to lead the students astray.

When I told Marjorie and her husband that you are Jewish, William said that Adventists feel a special connection to Jews since they share the same Sabbath. One of the Adventists' fundamental beliefs is to observe the Sabbath on the day the Bible designates (and as the Jews do) – Friday sunset to Saturday sunset. If I call William and Marjorie during that time, I'll get their voice mail. Staying off the phone is just one of many things they don't do on the Sabbath. It reminds me a bit of the Danans in San Antonio.

By the way, I'm going to be their soprano soloist for the Atlantic Union College performance of Haydn's Creation *– brings back memories of our wedding. At least it's a piece to which both of our religions can relate.*

Love,

Gayle

འ⟨⟩

April 25, 1993

Dear Harold,

She barely cleared your navel, but her slight frame contained a tow-ering spirit. Countless people came up to you to say how much your music touched them. But sometimes a piece of music is meant for just one person.

Her words will forever be etched in my memory. "You captured every emotion people felt in the Holocaust – and I'm saying that as someone who went through it." I had goose bumps thinking about what memories must have stirred inside this poor woman as she listened.

Those nights you sat at the piano creating this music, my mind many times drifted back to Anne Frank. I had thought about her so often when I was a girl. My childhood self couldn't imagine that someone of her tender age managed to preserve her humanity, her innocence and even her teenage longings while the world around her was swallowing thousands of Jews every day.

I don't understand how these people, who never knew if they would see the next sunrise, clung to their will to live. What strength came from their souls that gave them the hope to try for one more day, for one more hour to hold onto life?

For a long time, I couldn't sing the last song without breaking into tears.

I believe in God, even when He is silent.

It's not difficult to have faith when your greatest stress is the long line at the supermarket checkout. But when you see mothers torn from their children, husbands and wives separated for the rest of their short lives, people stripped of clothing, hair shorn, thrown into cattle cars, their very identity stolen by the most wicked and heartless oppressors in history – and some still managed to believe that God exists, and where that was not possible, to have faith in each other. And like Anne Frank, to still believe that "people are really good at heart."

I believe in God, even when He is silent.

That's why it was so important for you to end your piece with these words. It would be too easy to convey only despair, and despair was of course not unknown in the camps – how could it be otherwise? But if these monstrously abused victims could endure the greatest suffering imaginable and still believe that God was there, then why is it so hard for people whose faith is barely tested? Is it only in adversity, or catastrophe, that we can discover faith?

Of one thing I am certain after reading the survivors' poetry and singing your songs – if a Jew is forced to suffer the worst atrocity ever devised by mankind and come out of it still having a relationship with the Creator, then Anne Frank was right to place her faith in humanity despite everything.

Love,

Gayle

September 26, 1993

Dear Gayle,

Okay, this is weird, weird, weird. I get a gig this year singing in the Ohabei Shalom choir for the High Holidays. For all
the times I've sung in churches, this is my first synagogue gig.
As a Jew, I found the church gigs all by myself, and they even
found me a couple of times. But the synagogue gig – that one I
happened upon only because my non-Jewish wife is already singing there.

That's only the beginning of weird – after that it moves over
to bizarre. In college, I worked in a restaurant. Quickly, I discovered that a restaurant looks very different – and not in a positive
way – from the vantage point of the kitchen than it does as a guest
sitting out front at a table.

And so it was sitting with the choir behind the wall instead of
with the congregation. There were, of course, those same feelings
of isolation that you had described. But it's hard to even try to feel
a part of the service when half of the singers around you are reading the latest John Grisham novel or writing letters until it's time
to sing.

I believe that hiring me was part of the temple's affirmative
action plan. They noticed that the temple choir had no Jews, and
so I became the token Jew. I hope they don't try that with the
clergy.

So there I am, watching people reading and writing while the
service is going on across the wall, wondering what it means that
I am feeling like a distinct minority while sitting in the middle of
a synagogue. Then I smell something – a distinct lunchmeat odor
that I remember from my high school cafeteria, but whose identity evades me for the moment. And then I hear it – *crunch, crunch,
crunch*. And then, I look up, and I see it – the tenor is eating a ham
and cheese sandwich, on white bread with lettuce, mayonnaise
dripping out the sides.

I look at my watch – 12:00 – lunchtime.
But it's also Yom Kippur!

Love,

Harold

ॐ॰ॐ

May 18, 1994

Dear Gayle,

I once read that we shouldn't experience too many life changes within one year, as it can cause undue stress. Sometimes, life
gives you the changes anyway.

I love the new house. Our first house together, and I never
thought we'd own a Victorian. But to have moved just a month ago,
and have Law School graduation this weekend, and then start at a
downtown law firm in a couple of months – I'm beginning to feel
dizzy. I'm still not sure I want to practice law for the rest of my life,
but this will be a good chance to try it out.

Being a musician at an open-minded Catholic law school is
making for an interesting graduation. Friday night, I'm singing the
Kiddush at a special service organized for the Jewish students. And
it was one of the Jesuit priests who found a rabbi for us. Then Sunday morning, the law school is having a graduation Mass, and I'm
singing again. Obviously not the Kiddush.

By the way, my father asked if any other Jews live in our new
neighborhood. I don't think so, but it's a nice neighborhood, so I'm
not sure why that matters.

Love,

Harold

ॐ॰ॐ

May 24, 1995

Dear Harold,

Eastern Nazarene College has asked me to teach voice this fall. So now I'll work at two Christian schools run by, shall we say, not-in-the-mainstream denominations. As my mother remarked, I've gotten to know some of the more interesting corners of Christianity.

Like the Seventh Day Adventists, the Nazarenes are theologically conservative. Unlike the Seventh Day Adventists, the Nazarenes still hold their Sabbath on Sunday. Like the Seventh Day Adventists, the Nazarenes forbid alcohol. Unlike the Seventh Day Adventists, they eat meat. I hope I'm able to keep straight what's allowed and what's not as I zigzag between the two.

Oh, and Happy Anniversary – that is, for our first year in the new house. Yes, it's been a year.

A year since we bought our first house together. A year since you graduated law school. Almost a year since you began working at the law firm (even though you hate it, it's a great job for paying the bills).

Time isn't supposed to fly by this fast. But I feel like we're on a good path. The house is far bigger and more gorgeous than I imagined our finances could manage. And this area of Boston is like stepping into a 19th Century postcard with its Victorian homes and tree-lined streets.

The other day, a couple of miles from here, I noticed a Christian school with Stars of David in the masonry. A neighbor told me that the area was Jewish in the 1960s. So you're about thirty years behind the curve.

Love,

Gayle

చిళ

September 13, 1995

Dear Gayle,

Commas and capitalization – that's how I'm spending my days. I entered law school unsure whether I wanted to practice law. Now I know.

The other day, I was chastised for a misplaced comma in a brief. Better for the comma to be properly placed, I agree. A marking to that effect on the draft and one stroke of the keyboard, and we're done. Or we could be done, if this were anywhere but a law firm. Instead, I was treated to a fifteen-minute tour-de-force on comma placement – for which the partner is billing the client at a handsome rate.

Just as I thought I had grasped proper comma etiquette, I was blindsided by the capitalization conundrum. In another brief, I had listed the firm's name in capital letters, as the managing partner prefers. But a second partner working on the case reviewed the brief and has different capitalization preferences. I was hastily summoned to his office.

"Why did you put our firm's name in capital letters?" The partner looked like a cat about to pounce. "I was asked to do it that way. I thought this was the standard way our firm did it," I murmured, half-staring at my shoes and trying to give the impression that I thought this mattered more than all the starving children in Africa.

Let the pounce begin. "I must explain to you how this looks. There's a critical reason our firm's name needs to be in lower case. We're not grandstanding. We're not telegraphing our sense of importance. If we were to submit the firm's name capitalized, I can only imagine the judge's reaction." I beheld images of the judge, shocked and shaking, ripping up the brief before our eyes and demanding that we resubmit it in lower-case.

And so it went – another lecture billed to the client.

And to what end am I enduring this torture? The managing partner never fails to remind us that we're just like doctors in the operating room. Our client's fate will sink or swim based on what we do.

Except that we're nothing like doctors. The only fate hanging in the balance is that of our corporate client's insurance company, who may need to pay should the corporation they are insuring lose the case.

Some of the lawyers I've met are brilliant. And a few even do meaningful work. I just don't love it nearly enough to attempt that climb to the top and try to find a niche for myself that's semi-interesting.

What I'm doing isn't real. I need something real. And if not real, then at least tolerable.

Love,

Harold

&c&

Part III
The Search . . .

All the world is a very narrow bridge.
But the main thing is not to fear at all.

Rabbi Nachman of Breslov

February 2, 1996

Dear Harold,

"Okay, we've done those things. What's next?" I thought I might have heard you wrong as you finished glaring at our photo collage and then drifted out of the room. The last six years of our lives, and you think all we have to show for it is that we've done those things, and now what?

I've been hearing this for months. You feel something is missing. Your life lacks meaning. It feels shallow. You want something more than the "same old, same old."

All of your brooding is telling me there's a gap between us that I never suspected existed. I don't want to believe the gap is there. When I look at it, I wonder how it came to be. I'm not even sure what it is, or what to do about it. And I'm growing fearful.

I think we have a great life. You graduated from law school, cum laude no less, and landed a job with a prestigious Boston law firm. I know, I know – it's not your dream job, you want to run as fast as you can, but you don't know to where. But maybe things will get better. Maybe you'll find a different job. Maybe you'll find a more satisfying field – plenty of other lawyers have. You're acting like you've signed on as an indentured servant for the next thirty years, when you could be focusing on where you want to go from here rather than how awful everything is.

And not everything is awful. We bought a great house. Few people right out of law school are living in a 2,800 square foot Victorian in the heart of Boston. We have two darling cats and a one-in-a-million dog. I'm teaching at two good colleges, have a nice church gig, and am doing a fair amount of performing.

I'm growing fearful that it's more than the job. None of those collage photos had a thing to do with your job, yet they don't give you a bit of satisfaction.

So what's missing? I wish you'd open up to me – give me something more specific than your still-undefined quest for meaning. Say you regret marrying me, you think something's wrong with our relationship, you're now regretting your decision not to have children. In a rush to fill your silence, these are the thoughts going through my mind. Maybe it's none of these things. But I don't know, because you're not saying.

I want to help you sort through this, however I can. I love you more than you can imagine. You have so much to offer – as a husband, as a friend, as a musician, as a Jew, as a lawyer (yes, even as a lawyer).

Please open up and let me help you.

Love,

Gayle

ھۄ

February 8, 1996

Dear Gayle,

I didn't mean to imply that we've done nothing. Or that nothing about our lives is fulfilling. I know we have much to be grateful for.

Still, I do have this feeling that something is missing. At least, I don't want either of us to regret something once it is too late to do anything about it. And yes, that something is children.

A few days before I "glared" at our photos, (although I would characterize my expression as "reflective") I was singing at the Church of the Redeemer. I admit it's not the most enjoyable church gig I've had, and I'm not sure why I'm still giving up my Sunday mornings for it. As I sat there, enduring the overly-formal Episcopal service, I grew depressed.

The choir director and her husband had a baby a few months ago. I watched them each cradle him in their arms, their faces radiating a certain kind of love that I imagine only a parent and child share. At that moment, I wanted to feel what they felt. I wanted to have what they had.

I passed through the door of the warm sanctuary, taking in the snow-covered ground just beyond, the bite of the wind stinging my face. And I felt a hole in our lives.

I know that when we married, we both said we would never have children. One of the challenges in any marriage is that people change. As the years pass, the couple's feelings even about important life issues – especially about important life issues – are no longer the same.

I'm not trying to make up new ground rules. I'm not saying we must have kids. I couldn't say that anyway, as I'm pretty sure this is a decision that requires your consent. You still may not want children. I'm not yet absolutely sure I do. But I think the time has come to discuss the possibility.

Love,

Harold

ॐॐ

February 10, 1996

Dear Harold,

At least now I know what's bothering you. Having children is the biggest decision we could make. A child will change our lives beyond recognition – forever.

I've never thought much about having children of my own. I was always content to teach other people's children. As the idea begins to settle in, though, I'm not necessarily opposed.

I'm not in favor either. I don't know. I need time to think.

Life with children is not all about looking at a baby, your "face radiating a certain kind of love." You walked away from that couple and felt a hole in our lives. They walked away with diapers to change, scheduled feedings to which all other priorities must bend, and cries in the middle of the night that are oblivious to an adult's need for sleep. And as children grow, the problems grow with them. I have yet to meet a parent who is not beset with worry about one or another of their children.

I've also yet to meet a parent who doesn't think the inconveniences are worth it. And I must say, I think we could be pretty good at it.

Then, there's the religion issue. I already know, without discussing it, that you'd feel uncomfortable raising a child as a Christian. And I've never thought about what it would be like to raise a Jewish child.

It wouldn't be simple. I don't know how my parents would react to that little piece of news that a baptism is not in their grandchild's future. I don't know how I would explain to a child that we are raising him or her as a Jew, but that I sing and play for churches. And while we're at it, you would need to think about how you would explain why you're uncomfortable taking a child to church services, but are entirely comfortable singing in them.

I have no interest in raising a child in two religions, nor do you. But even if we raise a child in one religion, it's too easy in an interfaith household to send mixed signals. Whatever we do, I would want the child to feel rock-solid secure in his or her religious identity. It's much better if a child can say unambiguously, "I'm Jewish," or "I'm Christian," or "I'm Muslim." "I'm Jewish, but . . ." is not an ideal outcome.

Lots of intermarried parents love having the ". . ." It makes them feel like they are passing on some of their own religious tradition, even if their religion didn't "win" in the "how will we raise him" contest. But if we're to have a child, then religious upbringing needs to be about the child, not about us.

I'm getting ahead of myself. The first question is whether children fit into my world and into ours. And my answer is still that I don't know.

Too many people have children without even thinking. That's why there's no shortage of bad parenting, and more tragically, child abuse and neglect. I want us to take our time. Whatever our decision, we need to be fully at peace with it.

Love,

Gayle

৵৽

November 15, 1996

Dear Gayle,

I'm about to become what is called a "recovering lawyer." Young Audiences is an organization that brings performing arts programs into schools around Massachusetts. They need a director who can work with the performers, negotiate the contracts, promote the programs to schools, and manage the organization. And they've hired me!

The job fits perfectly with my combined music and law backgrounds. It's interesting. It's challenging. It's something I believe in.

Time to do something meaningful for a change.

Love,

Harold

୨ଏ

February 1, 1997

Dear Gayle,

Four of us sit behind the organ in the temple's orange-carpeted sanctuary every Friday night. I make my way to the microphone every so often, assuming my role as the Cantorial soloist. The other three provide the vocal back-up, popping into the congregation's view at key moments like a three-headed jack-in-the-box. In between, the rabbi coaxes the congregation to mumble through the responsive readings.

With nearly 1,000 families, it's the largest Reform temple in Newton, and one of the largest in the Boston area. At first, I thought it was much smaller, given that 50-75 people pass through its doors on a typical Friday night. In any of the churches where I've sung with a congregation this size, they would easily draw several hundred people every Sunday.

Other than a handful of regulars, each Friday night brings a new crowd, breaking from their High Holidays-only routine to say Kaddish for a departed relative. I wonder if coming to temple only when there is a relative to mourn reduces Judaism to a kind of ancestor worship.

A few additional pre-teens, and sometimes their parents, show up because the temple requires them to put in a set number of appearances before their Bar or Bat Mitzvah. I rarely see these families again once the big day has passed.

A moveable wall separates the sanctuary from the social hall, allowing for an expanded space that accommodates the swelled ranks for the High Holidays. On Friday nights, the wall remains in place, and that slightly overdone coffee smell that seems to pervade most temples welcomes people to the social hall for the Oneg Shabbat after services.

The four of us used to walk to the Oneg together. But no one talked to us, huddled instead in their private conversations. The organist even tried to introduce us to a few of the congregants, but most walked away shortly after the obligatory hello. My longest conversation was with a woman who, without a trace of a smile, told me that she would prefer if I sang one of the songs more slowly.

We stuck with it, trying to mingle with the congregation after the service. But after a few more Friday nights of standing in isolation, we started heading for our cars the minute the service was over. If this is how they treat the singers who they see leading the service, I can only imagine what happens when a newcomer visits.

All the churches were just places where I sang for a fee, although where people at least were friendly. The temple is now reduced to nothing more than singing for a fee, although where people can barely manage a hello. But this is not just a gig – it's my religion. I had expected more.

Love,

Harold

February 2, 1997

Dear Harold,

The one Friday night I followed you to services, I experienced the same thing. Except that only thirty people showed up for that service.

What I find hilarious is that the temple insists the Cantorial Soloist be Jewish. If you remember, when their organist was first looking for a singer to lead the service, he approached me, making certain assumptions because of my Jewish last name. When he learned otherwise, he cut off the conversation and rushed away as if I had some lethal disease.

Before this revelation, he was ready to hire me even though I don't read Hebrew. Even though I work in a church. Even though I wouldn't understand the words I'm singing. But my non-Jewish pedigree renders me ineligible, and apparently I wouldn't qualify even if I were a non-Jewish Hebrew scholar.

More ironically, the organist is not Jewish, nor are the other three singers. But the person they trot out front must be Jewish. I could understand if they were a congregation that follows Jewish tradition. But when Friday night reminds me of a Unitarian service, the congregants don't seem to know the prayers, and you're one of the only people in the room even wearing a kippah, I find their "Jewish-only" rule astounding.

From the outside, it looks like they are more interested in window dressing than in Jewish substance.

Love,

Gayle

৵৵

April 8, 1997

Dear Harold,

Children have been on my mind these past few months, ever since you brought it up. I go back and forth. The joy of a child's smile – diapers. The

*artwork proudly displayed on the refrigerator – a career on hold. Hearing
the child's first words – midnight feedings. The first piano lesson – how to
resolve the religion issue.*

*Yesterday, riding the subway on my way to teach, I played this ping
pong game yet again. And then something in the corner of my eye caught my
attention. The mental chatter retreated, and suddenly I knew.*

*She appeared about my height. Her hair was similar to mine. In
fact, she looked enough like me that I readily saw myself in her. She was
gazing at a magazine, an article about planning the baby's nursery. A
photo displayed the kind of crib that shows up more often in these magazines than in real life. A set of matching blankets hung over the side of
the crib, while nearby stood a dresser, changing table, and built-in toy
cabinet.*

*For a moment, I dismissed the magazine fairy tale, retreating again
to my now-familiar back and forth.*

*But only for a moment. I watched her eyes drinking in this image of
her future, her stomach revealing that that was only a month or two away.
I watched her face, dreaming and hoping.*

*My doubts didn't vanish. But in that instant, I thought about when
we first met, when we told each other that our love would overcome everything. As I exited the subway car, I said to myself that we can do this too,
that we'll find a way.*

Love,

Gayle

᠊ᢀᥬ᠊

April 9, 1997

Dear Gayle,

If we both really want this, then the way will appear. The
minute I started wanting children, I was so afraid you didn't. Then
I kept questioning whether I really did, or whether it was just the
idea that I liked when I saw other people with children.

We'll share all of it – the baby's first words and the piano lessons, and the diaper changes and the temper tantrums. Oh, and I promise we'll get a really nice crib.

Love,

Harold

ॐॐ

October 27, 1997

Dear Harold,

The doctor's words still sting in my ears. All those years that I didn't want a child, I never thought a child might not want me. I didn't imagine that I might not be able to have a baby. Now I long for one.

That woman I saw on the subway is holding her baby in her arms by now. What about me? All that complaining about diaper changes, and now it all seems so trivial.

I'll have to find a way to come to terms with this. But right now, it hurts too much.

Love,

Gayle

ॐॐ

December 5, 1997

Dear Gayle,

How did we come to spend our days dreaming of a child? We, who dreamed of careers and houses and music and a long life together – but never of a child.

It appears the dream isn't going away. It's settled in, made itself right at home. It screams at us when we walk by the empty room that's the perfect size for a nursery. It taunts us when we walk out to the silent back yard that's meant to hold a child's laughter. It seizes us in an unyielding grip when we notice the game of tag across the street.

The dream is talking – no – demanding. Demanding that we either banish it from our lives, or do something to fulfill it. If having a child biologically isn't in the cards, then the only way to fulfill the dream is to adopt. Or to cast the dream away.

Love,

Harold

᷈᷈

March 23, 1998

Dear Harold,

At long last, the ping pong game in my mind is over. For months, it was back and forth, back and forth, have a child, don't have a child.

Conclusion of round one – have a child.

Then I learned I had to play with a different paddle. Back and forth, back and forth, adopt, don't adopt.

Conclusion of round two – the bottom line is that I want a child.

I'm reading An Empty Lap *by Jill Smolowe. After a couple hundred pages describing her and her husband's own ping pong game, she tells of their journey to China to adopt a baby. Toward the book's close, she is watching her husband playing with their now two-year-old daughter. As the author's eyes shift from one to the other, an American man and a Chinese girl, she can't help but see a resemblance between father and daughter.*

Such an innocent observation. But it cut right through me. I put down the book and thought for a long time about what being a parent really means. Giving birth is necessary to bring a child into the world. It doesn't make one a parent, however. To be a parent is to raise a child. It's about instilling values. It's about giving all of yourself to help your child find his place in the world. It's about tending to all those wounds of childhood – the little cuts and scrapes, and the deeper ones that hurt inside. It's about being there for your child through good and bad, no matter what. None of that has a thing to do with giving birth.

I'm ready to be a parent.

Love,

Gayle

৵৹

August 16, 1998

Dear Harold,

This morning brought me back to that day eight years ago when a woman from the Midwest tied the knot with a guy from the East Coast. Everything had a familiar ring as I looked at the Christians and Jews gathered together in the white-walled box of a room, the groom from Philadelphia waiting anxiously, and the bride from Farmington – this time my sister Angela – walking down the aisle. They did manage to convince a rabbi and a minister to appear together, avoiding our Justice of the Peace route.

Statistically, what are the chances that in a family of four children growing up in a tiny Christian farming town 20 miles from Peoria, Illinois, and going to church every Sunday, two of them would marry Jews?

Love,

Gayle

৵৹

November 5, 1998

Dear Gayle,

"Honey, please sit down, I have something to tell you. Remember how . . . when we talked about . . . I said . . . we had planned . . . uh, well . . . honey, we're going to have a baby."

None of those conversations for us. We researched the options. We decided to adopt from Russia. We called to make an appointment with the lady from Maine Adoption Placement Service. We sat in the waiting area, nervously reading parenting magazines to pass the time. We met for two hours – questions, what if, how to. And we left with a mountain of paperwork to complete that would leave any biological parent reeling.

But we're going to be parents! All we have to do is fill out dozens of forms, submit to a multi-visit evaluation by a social worker and then to a local criminal background check and then to a Federal one (including fingerprints), attend training sessions, procure official copies of every single vital document of our lives starting with our birth certificates and going to the present day, get apostilles for each document so that they're acceptable internationally, get all the documents translated for the Russian authorities, fill out the Russian paperwork, wait for an indeterminate period until we're matched with a child, fly to Russia, shuttle between Russian government offices to ensure our paperwork is in order, appear before a Russian judge and be grilled on why we want to take this child to America, wait for hours at the American Embassy in Moscow to process more paperwork, and then appear in a U.S. court upon our return to finalize everything.

Yes, only a few short steps stand between us and parenthood.

Love,

Harold

෩෨

March 12, 1999

Dear Gayle,

"We will raise our child Jewish."

You said it so matter-of-factly that even your parents reacted as if it were obvious and there were no other options. As I looked at you, and then your parents, and then mine, I seemed to be the only one in the room who was surprised.

We had barely discussed how we would raise this child. From the time we met, we both knew that if we had children, we would raise them in just one religion. But we never did agree on what that religion would be.

Ever since deciding to adopt, we've skirted around this issue. I've wanted to resolve it, but dreaded the land mines it might expose, not knowing exactly where you stood. Now I know.

I admit I'm relieved. I'm relieved that the conversation I dreaded is not necessary. I'm relieved that you still think a child should be raised in only one religion. And I'm relieved that we agree. I'm not quite sure how we got here, though.

The "one religion per child" rule was never in doubt. More typically, interfaith couples hold elaborate negotiations around this issue. Perhaps our clarity in those early days arose from our equally strong conviction that we would never be raising a child.

Having observed more than a few intermarried families over the years, I know our first intuition was correct. I think of the two musicians from Young Audiences – Karen's Jewish, Tom was raised as a Christian. They've consciously excluded religion from their own lives, and that's how they're raising their child. At least they're consistent. Yet, watching them, and especially their son – something is missing.

Then there is the couple who is sending their children to the Hebrew school at Temple Israel *and* to the church school at All Saints Episcopal. The double dose must be taxing, and I wonder just where all that intense carpooling is leading. Their children are learning that Judaism and Christianity share certain beliefs and values. They're also learning that Jesus is the Messiah in one building on one day, but isn't the Messiah across town on another.

The parents I've met who raise their children in both insist they are teaching open-mindedness, tolerance, sharing in what each religion has to offer, and so forth. But each parent can be open-minded about the other religion precisely because they identify unambiguously with their own. They are grounded in one place, and reach out from that place. Yet they force their children to shuttle between two spiritual homes, never staying in one for very long. They deny their children the same single-religion grounding that they enjoy.

The children can always decide when they grow up, or so the thinking goes. But I wonder if this "try before you buy" approach substitutes the parents' feelings for the child's best interests. I recently had lunch with Michael, a Young Audiences board member. Michael is Catholic, his first wife is Jewish, and they exposed their son to both. Now 15, their son has gravitated toward Judaism and decided to have a Bar Mitzvah

Michael supports his son's decision, but his eyes betrayed a certain sadness as he spoke of it. I asked him whether his son felt as if he were choosing one parent over the other. "Yes, very definitely," he said without pausing. He told me of his son's guilt feelings, and how he worked hard to convince his son that choosing Judaism would not affect their relationship.

Then Michael's voice rose a bit as he said, "If I were to do it over again, I would raise my son in only one faith. It's better in the long run."

Indeed. Parents decide what clothes their young children will wear, what food they will eat, and when they will go to bed. Yet when it comes to their spiritual life, their identity, how they view their place in this world, everything can be deferred until they're safely out of the house?

And that brings me back to your decision to raise our child as a Jew. I'm not only relieved. I'm grateful. But I'm also a tad wary. We'll need to figure out together exactly what this means, beyond taking the child to synagogue instead of church.

In terms of our home, it's not so straightforward. Judaism is centered on the home much more than is Christianity. Our home, until now, has not been overtly Jewish or Christian. There is no Christmas tree. Nor is there a mezuzah on the doorpost. If we are raising a Jewish child, we'll need to decide how this will play out in our home. I want our child's religious upbringing to be a source of joy – for all of us.

Love,

Harold

శ్రిళ్ళ

March 14, 1999

Dear Harold,

I hadn't thought about a mezuzah on the doorpost, or specifically what will be Jewish about our home beyond raising a Jewish child in it. I haven't thought what it will be like to raise a Jewish child while working as the Organist/Choir Director for United Church in Walpole. I haven't thought about finding a temple that we will both like and will accommodate a family like ours.

There probably are a million other things I need to think through, and I don't even know what they are. All I know is that raising our child as a Jew seems right. Call it women's intuition. Other than that, I can't tell you why.

I know we're not taking a well-traveled road. But have we ever?

Love,

Gayle

శ్రిళ్ళ

September 21, 1999

Dear Harold,

"Is the cat out of the bag yet?"
It's not every Yom Kippur that a rabbi has welcomed us with this particular greeting. Then again, not every rabbi would let you chant "Kol Nidre" when he had never heard you sing a note, and then agree to keep it a secret from your parents.

This Yom Kippur left everyone surprised. "Uh . . . yes, of course . . . three times?" I could almost hear the wheels turning inside your head as Rabbi Loeb sidled up to you with this little piece of news just a few minutes before the service began. "'Kol Nidre' . . . uh, you repeat it . . . uh . . . three times . . . yes, of course . . . is it ok if Gayle plays the second repetition as an organ solo? It will make it easier for me if I can take a break in the middle." You can thank me for acting as if, yes, I had planned all along to play a five minute organ solo in the middle of "Kol Nidre" – I thought I was going to faint!

The moment you began, any lingering uncertainty faded away. Your singing pierced the air with a special quality I hadn't heard from you before. But your Mom's and Dad's faces said it all.

I found myself on an emotional roller coaster of my own. At the memorial service, the woman who handed me a tissue as I got teary-eyed might have taken a dimmer view had she known that the loved ones I was mourning were our dog and cat who had both died a month before. In the absence of a child, they were like children to us.

At least the Torah reading gave me a chuckle. When Rabbi Loeb called "Mr. and Mrs. Harold Berman" up front to recite the blessings over the Torah, my first thought was that maybe there's another Mr. and Mrs. Harold Berman in the congregation. But when he looked in our direction and motioned for us to come forward, I thought, "Okay – deep breath – I've heard this done before. I'll get through it." A man pointed to a piece of paper with Hebrew and English on it. I stared at it blankly. As we lurched into the blessings, I just smiled and pretended like I knew what I was doing, mouthing whatever words I could remember and hiding my voice behind yours. Everything, including the fast, was a breeze after that.

You were right to insist we go to the Monroe Temple this year. Families should be together for as many holidays as possible. Next year may we come to Monroe with a child in our arms!

Love,

Gayle

৵৵

September 22, 1999

Dear Gayle,

Yes, the *Kol Nidre* three times rule was a new one for me. There's so much I don't know.

The greater shock was when Rabbi Loeb called us up to say the blessing over the Torah. I guess no one tipped off the rabbi that we are intermarried. When he asked for your Hebrew name, all I could do was mumble, "She doesn't have a Hebrew name," which I suppose was the best thing to say under the circumstances. It wasn't our fault. He assumed that, if I was singing *Kol Nidre*, and you were playing the organ for me, then we must both be Jewish. Ah, appearances can be deceiving.

Your accolades mean the world to me. My father said that people really responded, and even the teenagers in the back stopped talking and turned to listen. I thought such an occurrence only happens when the Messiah comes.

Seriously, something came out in my singing from deep within, something I've never felt before. I'm calling it "something" because I can't say what it was. Unlike the countless times I've sung in synagogues and churches as if I were giving a performance, this time it had nothing to do with my voice, my singing, my ego, or even about conveying the emotions of the *Kol Nidre*. It was beyond all that.

"Du-du-du-du – you have just entered the Twilight Zone." I hope this doesn't sound too out there – but I can only describe this something as an encounter with a "Presence." It was subtle, hovering just out of range, but unmistakably there. It surrounded me. It saturated every note I sang. When I reached the finish, I felt like a wrung-out dishtowel, strangely at peace.

Whatever this "something" was, I now feel like I am standing on the opposite side of a threshold – and what that threshold is, I don't know. But everything seems just a bit different from before.

Even little things like the rabbi's sermon. Commonplace messages that before would have drifted past me, all of a sudden are clamoring for my attention.

Rabbi Loeb's theme has become almost a mantra intoned from countless High Holiday pulpits across America. In essence – "We're glad you're here, but please don't disappear until next year's High Holidays. Judaism and our temple exist for more than two days a year. Try Shabbat."

These sermons always mask a certain desperation. The rabbi knows he has twenty minutes to wow hundreds of bored people who have no intention of doing anything other than disappearing until next year.

I'm not sure why so many rabbis persist in this folly. Not only do most of their congregants go AWOL until the following year. Many walk out to avoid hearing the sermon.

Perhaps the rabbis hope that someone out there will listen and decide to make a change. This year, that someone was me.

Rabbi Loeb began by stating what would be painfully obvious in any setting other than the average temple. "You have twenty-five hours. What you put into the next twenty-five hours will determine what you get out of them."

My mind simultaneously gasped "Aha!" and "Duh!"

Painfully obvious, yet I've missed it all this time. Although I suspect I'm in good company on that one.

Try playing clarinet twice a year and see how unbearable it sounds. Or try the twice-a-year method with running, astrophysics, golf, or anything else.

Most Jews, myself included, treat Judaism as the great exception to this rule. We all talk so self-righteously about our Jewish identity, as if talking without doing actually means something. As if Jewish food, Jewish humor, and a generic feeling of belonging to the "tribe" can overcome our not having a clue about Jewish texts, Jewish history or Jewish prayer.

I don't know where I've been all of these years. I've talked about delving more into Judaism. I've had opportunities to go deeper. But I've done very little.

Maybe I'm a tad resentful at the Jewish world too, or at least the one of Hebrew school carpools, Bar Mitzvahs that could feed a starving African nation, and yes, twice-a-year synagogue appearances. Most of us couldn't speak coherently about our purpose as Jews if our lives depended on it.

My little foray into *Kol Nidre* tells me there's far more to Judaism than I can yet imagine. I can't walk away anymore.

Don't worry – I'm not going to go off and become a fanatic. I'm not sure what I'm going to do. I'll get back to you.

Love,

Harold

ॐ

September 24, 1999

Dear Harold,

Christianity also has its twice-a-year attendees. They show up on Christmas Eve and Easter Sunday. When I was at Colonial Hills Church, we dubbed them the "C & E" crowd. I've also wondered why people bother going just those two times and are nowhere to be found the rest of the year. I don't know what they get out of it.

Some people go to make their parents happy, and some go to see the church all decked out on Christmas and Easter. Some go because they like the holiday music. Some, probably most, go because they feel they should "do something."

So the rest of us who work hard and faithfully go to services each week have to put on an even bigger show for these people who couldn't care less if the church exists the other 363 days. I've always felt they would do just as well to stay home and have a party. In fact, that's clearly what some of them do before sliding into the Christmas Eve service. I have, more than once, been playing organ while someone nearby is acting as if he's still at a nightclub.

But many ministers believe that if they can get the C & E crowd to walk in the door, then they have a chance of "reaching" them. The rabbis are doing the same thing on the High Holidays. Sometimes, it even works – like with you and Rabbi Loeb. Maybe everything the staff and clergy put up with is worth it if they touch even one soul.

I agree with you. Practicing Judaism (or any religion) is similar to playing an instrument – something done occasionally will never hold the same meaning as something that becomes integral to your life. The Christians I have known who get the most out of Christianity are not the C & E crowd, or even the ones who only attend church on Sunday mornings. They are the ones who also go to Bible classes, study on their own and give of themselves by living the values they are learning.

But I think Judaism is fighting a tougher battle than Christianity. In addition to religion, Judaism has the "peoplehood" issue. This gives Jews a wonderful dimension that Christians don't have. But it also gives them an easy out.

There are some whose sole claim to Christianity is Christmas gifts and Easter eggs. But as a rule, a person who grew up going to church but no longer believes in God is not called a Christian. He's called an atheist. However, a Jew who grew up going to synagogue but no longer believes in God is still called a Jew.

In Judaism, you're either born a Jew or decide to convert. I imagine that some Jews would like to run as far as they can from Judaism, so they don't have to feel guilty about not doing Jewish things. But even if they take on another religion, does that mean they are no longer Jewish? I've heard of Jewish Buddhists, Jewish atheists, even Jewish Christians – it seems impossible for them to shake the Jewish part. Or perhaps they don't want to, even as they practice a different religion.

They can always fall back on the peoplehood part to give them an easy excuse when it comes to not grappling with the religion part. But if someone already belongs to a religion because they were born into it, they may as well make the effort to learn as much as they can and see if there's something meaningful in it. If they are going to move to another faith – or to no faith at all – they at least ought to know what they are giving up.

No matter which religion, though, if a person isn't willing to put in the work, then they're not going to find much about it that's attractive.

Have fun exploring . . .

Love,

Gayle

☙❧

September 27, 1999

Dear Gayle,

I feel funny asking you this, but what kind of synagogue are you looking for? I've haven't figured that one out either. So this morning, I called the Massachusetts Synagogue Council. The woman on the other end of the line suggested a few synagogues she thought might be a fit.

When I said I wanted a traditional Reform temple, she first suggested Ohabei Shalom. Yes, the same Ohabei Shalom where I was the token Jew in the High Holidays choir, accompanied by a tacky electronic synthesizer. When I offered that we were looking for something more traditional, she said that, for a Reform temple, Ohabei Shalom *is* traditional.

She told me about two other Reform temples, both twenty miles away, and then suggested we might try a Conservative temple if traditional is what we want.

Conservative scares me a little. The Reform movement is all I know. I like not having to worry about navigating through a maze of Hebrew I don't understand, or how people will respond to an interfaith couple in their midst.

Then again, we've tried several Reform temples over the years, and none have clicked. Whatever we decide, I want to feel comfortable, and you do too. But you and I may have different ideas about what it takes to feel comfortable. So what do you want from a synagogue?

Love,

Harold

ॐॐ

September 28, 1999

Dear Harold,

Since you're the Jew here, I think it's you who needs to be happy with the synagogue. Perhaps we can try a few Friday night services that are an easy drive. Something close by will make Hebrew school easier when the time comes. And yes, I can do without that cheesy synthesizer.

Love,

Gayle

ॐॐ

October 9, 1999

Dear Gayle,

Your face locked in a perpetual cringe – looking at your watch in disbelief – not happy with what you dubbed "the campfire songs." I get it. You didn't like the service. To be honest, the campfire songs didn't bother me so much.

Ever since coming to Boston, I've wanted to find a congregation where people are serious about spirituality. It's easy to find a synagogue that has a building fund, a High Holiday ticket policy, or vacuous conversations that eclipse the prayers. But spirituality? For some reason, that's not at the top of every synagogue's list. Except for Beth Am in San Antonio, I've left every synagogue we've tried feeling unchanged, and sometimes a bit deflated.

Whatever the quality of the songs, whatever the quality of the singing, whatever the key (or multiple keys simultaneously) in which they chose to sing, at least they sang with spirit. As with Beth Am, Temple Beth Zion seems to be a refuge for people who want to do more than read responsively, listen to political sermons, and sit comfortably in a service filled with lifelessness. They call it Jewish Renewal, and I've been told that it's all about bringing Judaism out of the doldrums.

This was the first place since moving to Boston where I felt I could try to get into the service unselfconsciously. Everywhere else, people went through the motions, and I would have looked and felt odd had I done something radical like singing the songs any louder than a mumble.

The Torah study proved to be even better than the service. People asked questions. People cared about what they were studying. They weren't afraid to challenge, to probe, to learn. That's what I want. I'm tired of places where I have to fight against the lethargy around me.

Like you, I also continue to grapple with the music issue. Jewish music doesn't have any Bachs or Beethovens – it leans heavily on folk tradition. I read that from the destruction of the Temple in Jerusalem until modern times, Jews traditionally did not use instruments on Shabbat. So Jewish music has had built-in limitations. I assume you would go just as crazy if you had to listen to nothing but Gregorian chant. It's nice and peaceful – for about five minutes. Still, even after Jews brought instruments into the service, no Bachs or Beethovens have been forthcoming.

But Bach and Beethoven still exist. I can pray at synagogue, and get my classical music experience elsewhere. Perhaps we differ because I fell in love with music independent of the synagogue whereas your musical life has often been connected to the church.

One thing about Friday night still bothers me, though. Nobody, except for the rabbi, said one word to us at the Oneg Shabbat. They all seemed to know each other and talked happily among themselves. But it never occurred to any of them to turn around and welcome two strangers who were standing awkwardly in the corner. How the congregants act after the service is at least as important as how enthusiastically they sing during the service.

Somewhere in Boston, there must be a congregation that is serious, that treats people nicely, and that has good music – or at least music we can live with.

Love,

Harold

જ્જ્જ

November 8, 1999

Dear Harold,

Temple Beth Zion's songs-around-the-campfire service was just the beginning. There was also the synagogue with the cantor whose voice inspired me – that is – to run from the room as fast as possible. There was the "high church" Reform temple, complete with a bad imitation of a church choir and organ. Then there was the synagogue where the talking never stopped. And the synagogue whose guitar-toting rabbi acted like he was auditioning for the next Peter, Paul & Mary trio.

Finding a congregation that's friendly has been hit or miss. But even where they were friendly, it's hard to get past a service that's uncomfortable. Another issue I've had during this whole "synagogue shopping" experience is that I don't know the songs – neither the words nor the music. And since, unlike a church, there's no music to read, it's next to impossible to learn the songs – especially when the people around me are either singing off-key or barely singing at all. I suppose if I go enough, the songs will start to sink in.

Perhaps the real reason I'm experiencing musical distress is that I'm used to being in charge of the music, not sitting in the pews. All of these years, I've been the one choosing which music is performed, not trying to decipher it from someone else's leaves-something-to-be-desired rendition.

Ultimately, my disappointment comes as much from being a professional singer and voice teacher than from any specific issues with synagogue music. If we were church shopping, I wouldn't be so easily appeased either (although, at least in a church, the music would be written down). I'm overly critical if the music isn't high quality. It's an occupational hazard.

Didn't the woman from the Synagogue Council recommend that small synagogue in Milton? I know it's Conservative, so we'll have to find out if they'll accept me. But it might be worth a try. It's a much closer drive than any of the other places, so if nothing else, it has convenience going for it. It may even have music going for it. Someone – I don't remember who – mentioned that they have a good cantor. If that's true, I could live with a lot of other things.

Love,

Gayle

⊰⊱

November 13, 1999

Dear Gayle,

No cringing face. No campfire songs. No looking at your watch. I think we're onto something.

Sometimes you search far and wide to find that what you were looking for was right under your nose. Temple Shalom has the good music you want. It has the friendly congregation I want.

As for the very traditional service – I worked so hard trying to keep up with the Hebrew, hoping people wouldn't notice that I had no clue what I was doing. At least I didn't hold the prayer book upside down. But all this struggling to follow the prayers left me little energy to try to connect with them.

Every so often I would take a break from my efforts and look around the congregation. Some were waiting impatiently for the service to finish and the congregational dinner in the social hall to start. Some appeared to be as lost as I was. And some prayed as if the prayers were old friends.

I'd love to be counted in that latter group, but it's a challenge when you're stealthily looking over the shoulder of the person in the next row to see if you're still (or ever were) on the right page.

Even though I feel incompetent, the traditional service has a certain authenticity that's appealing. No trying to be like a church service, or a rock concert. No trying to apologize for what it's not. The service doesn't grovel – it just tries to be itself.

And if I relax just a little, every once in a while the barrage of Hebrew gives way to a certain stillness, a stillness that invites me to something deeper than my everyday petty concerns. I could use more of that stillness in my life. It may be worth learning my way around the service to get it.

Love,

Harold

ॐ

November 17, 1999

Dear Harold,

At least you know enough Hebrew to worry about keeping up. I'm not worried at all – I couldn't begin to find my place in the service. I barely noticed the Hebrew anyway. I spent most of the time listening to the Cantor, and marveling that it's possible after all to find a synagogue with music that doesn't conjure up memories of an elementary school concert. The meaning of the prayers permeates his every note, even though I don't understand a word. And unlike just about every other synagogue we've been to, he sings in tune! Such a small thing to ask for, but it's in noticeably short supply.

I know there's more to a service, and certainly a congregation, than the music. But it's important to me. And besides, if I can enjoy the music rather than be distracted by it, then I can begin to focus on other things.

Speaking of which, whatever concerns I had about Conservative Jews accepting a non-Jew in their midst have been put to rest. At the din-

ner following the service, it seemed as if the people couldn't get to our table fast enough to welcome the new couple. I could not detect any concern about my religion. In fact, they are eager for me to participate. They even want me to join the sisterhood (I need to find out what that is first).

I didn't know what to expect when we met with Rabbi Fogel a few days later. At first, I was intimidated by the hundreds of books that wrapped around his office from floor to ceiling. But when he confided that it is often the non-Jewish spouse who shoulders the responsibility of getting the children to Hebrew School, I knew I could fit into this community.

I was kind of surprised, though, when he looked me in the eye and asked, "Have you ever considered converting?" My answer surprised me even more: "No, I couldn't because of my parents." Converting hasn't been on my mind, so it was strange to hear those words tumble from my mouth. Just as I began to feel a knot in my stomach, I was relieved to hear him say it didn't matter to him or the congregation, and that he is happy we have decided to raise our child as a Jew.

Rabbi Fogel says that our child's Conservative conversion will be accepted by virtually everyone, and there would only be an issue if he ever decided to become an Israeli citizen. I don't understand the ins and outs of Jewish conversion and why one type of conversion is accepted by some and not others. But this seems good enough for me. I can't imagine we'll ever be moving to Israel.

I'm glad we're finally done with synagogue shopping. This is probably as much "at home" as I could feel in a temple.

Love,

Gayle

౭ూక

December 16, 1999

Dear Harold,

I'm beginning to feel religiously schizophrenic. We go to Shabbat services on Friday night, and on Sunday I arrive at church ready to lead *the choir and play the organ. It's interesting to note the similarities and differences, but I'm trying to think of them as separate experiences so I can appreciate each for what it is.*

Little did I imagine that church and synagogue would come together at tonight's performance of Handel's Messiah *at Eastern Nazarene College. I arrived an hour early to rehearse my solos with the orchestra, only to learn that the mezzo-soprano was sick, and after a frantic search, they had found a substitute just fifteen minutes earlier. Luz walked in, ready to rehearse her arias. She was personable and had a nice voice. But the whole room was focusing on just one thing – imagine a mezzo-soprano, in the middle of an Evangelical Christian school, appearing before a rapt audience of hundreds of Evangelical Christians, singing words such as "Behold a virgin shall conceive and bear a son," all while sporting a large Star of David around her neck.*

The Evangelicals didn't know what to make of it. Several asked her if she was a Jews for Jesus. When she said that, no, she had grown up as a Christian but converted to Reform Judaism after she married a Jewish man, they became even more perplexed.

Luz felt bad, and asked me if she had done something wrong. I understand where the Evangelicals are coming from. Jews wouldn't be thrilled if a lapsed Jew walked into a synagogue wearing a cross. But I told her it was ok – she seemed so innocent and really didn't understand the problem. She wears the Star of David all the time, and she thought of this as just another performance. Perhaps if she had been singing with the local choral society rather than on an Evangelical college campus, it wouldn't have mattered.

Still, the juxtaposition of Handel's Messiah *with a Star of David is jarring.*

Love,

Gayle

ॐ✥

December 24 (Christmas Eve), 1999

Dear Gayle,

Tonight, I experienced a jarring juxtaposition of my own.

Last Shabbat, Rabbi Fogel reminded us that Christmas Eve and New Year's Eve would both fall on a Friday night this year. He pleaded with the congregation to keep the next two Friday nights for Shabbat, despite the siren song of tinsel and lights all around us. He even touched on the Jewish roots of Christianity, pointing out that New Year's Day is eight days after Christmas, which means it would have been the day of Jesus' circumcision. That certainly puts all of those New Year parties in a different light.

I wondered why he bothered, and if he had any idea of the vast insecurity he was conveying. Perhaps Jews would skip synagogue in favor of their New Year's Eve party. But very few (except for some interfaith families) would be at home trimming the tree the Friday before.

Then again, sometimes a message takes a while to hit home. When December 24th arrived, I showed up for Friday evening services, which I would have done even had the rabbi not taken the trouble to enlighten me about Jesus' circumcision. With the service starting just before sundown, I had plenty of time to get to the church for my 11 p.m. Christmas Eve gig. I hadn't been looking for this gig, but the church choir director desperately needed a baritone, and I didn't want to let her down.

The church, just a mile from Temple Shalom, is straight out of a Norman Rockwell painting. With its white wooden pews and stained glass, the sanctuary looks hardly different from when it was built thirty years before the Civil War. In the kitchen, the choir members huddled around cups of hot coffee, enjoying that special camaraderie that most church choirs seem to have.

When the clock struck eleven, we processed into the sanctuary, our maroon choir robes and our music illuminated only by the candle we each held.

"Once in David's royal city stood a lowly cattle shed," we intoned in a near-whisper as the organ weaved its way under our voices.

"Where a mother laid her baby in a manger for his bed."

My mind struggled, unable to shake the growing dissonance between where I was and where I had been just a few hours before.

"Mary, loving mother mild, Jesus Christ her little child." The congregation gradually joined in as we slowly made our way to the choir loft.

Finally, the processional ended. And in a moment never to be replicated in any synagogue, the entire congregation sat down in unison, uttering not a word.

When the time came for my solo, I forced a smile, hoping to mask the angst churning underneath. A few hundred people smiled back at me, their angelic expressions befitting what for them was the holiest night of the year.

I made it to the end of the solo, the large cross hovering on the wall behind me, competing only with the green and tinsel of the nearby Christmas tree. The minister spoke of Jesus' miraculous virgin birth, Joseph and Mary finding no room at the inn, and the message of universal peace for mankind.

We sang again: "Come to Bethlehem and see, Christ whose birth the angels sing; come, adore on bended knee, Christ the Lord, the newborn king."

And then, as we thundered the catchy finale, that angst grew into a gnawing voice, stridently insisting that this was still Friday night, still the Jewish Sabbath.

Joy to the world, the Lord is come! Let earth receive her king.

"Harold," the voice said, "Look at them. They wouldn't miss Christmas Eve for anything. And here you are, not missing it either, even for Shabbat – your Shabbat."

Let every heart prepare him room, and heaven and nature sing, and heaven and nature sing . . .

"Well, how does it feel to spend Shabbat in a church, singing about a virgin birth and all the rest that you don't believe? They believe it – that's why they're here. Care to remind me just why *you're* here?"

Joy to the world, the savior reigns! Let all their songs employ.

"A bit hypocritical, don't you think, to dismiss their beliefs when you're not acting on yours? What do you believe, anyway? Does Shabbat even matter to you – or only when you're spending it in a church? You keep saying you want to delve into Judaism. I have news for you – this doesn't cut it."

While field and floods, rocks, hills, and plains, repeat the sounding joy, repeat the sounding joy . . .

"Yeah, I know – you're not the only Jew in the world who doesn't observe Shabbat. But what kind of excuse is that? It's Friday night, a gift that Jews have been given for over 3,000 years. . .

Joy to the world, the Lord has come.

"Harold, it's Shabbat. What the hell are you doing here?"

For years, every time I've entered a church, I've convinced myself that I was just performing, just offering my services. Back in San Antonio, when I sang for your Palm Sunday service, Mike Yasenchak was onto something when he joked, "What's a nice Jewish boy like you doing in a place like this?" Only it's taken a while to sink in that it's no joke.

My intent is not to disparage Christians. Churches are designed just for them. I belong elsewhere. Showing up in a church – for pay – to sing words I don't believe in front of people who do is not open-minded. It's opportunistic.

And what have I gained? With all those years sitting in church, supposedly as just a job, I know more quotes from the New Testament than from the Torah. I can explain the Gospels better than I can the Talmud. Very tolerant of me to know all about Christianity without a clue about Judaism. Very pluralistic of me to hire myself out for Christmas Eve on Shabbat.

The people in the pews tonight proudly live their lives as Christians. The time has come for me to stop talking, and to start living my life as a Jew.

Love,

Harold

December 27, 1999

Dear Harold,

This weekend was a blur. It started on Friday afternoon with the Family Christmas service at United Church. Then I rehearsed with the choir, and then led them in the 11:00 Christmas Eve service. Saturday afternoon, I played organ for two Roman Catholic services with two different priests, both of whom, strangely enough, echoed Rabbi Fogel that New Year's Day is eight days from December 25 (although they didn't happen to mention the part about the circumcision). Then I dashed back to United Church to rehearse with the trumpet player for the two regular Sunday morning services, at which I played organ and directed the choir.

Finally, the Christmas season is over. All those extra rehearsals, performances of Handel's "Messiah," additional services and new music to learn. I've come to detest the glitz and tinsel of the season (not to mention the poorly performed Christmas carols) – and I'm exhausted.

But I don't have any of the feelings you do about performing in a church. Then again, I'm not Jewish. Then again, you've been performing in churches ever since I've known you, and these feelings are surfacing only now. I think I understand, though. You're discovering more about Judaism, and you're becoming more enthusiastic. This is making you feel conflicted. Sometimes, when Christians become more religious, they have a hard time reconciling their new selves with how they led their lives before.

But I suspect there's more to this than your new-found religious feelings. We will most likely be traveling to Russia in just a few months to adopt a little boy, who we will be raising as a Jew. We still haven't decided exactly what that involves, beyond synagogue membership and Hebrew school. But you know it doesn't include church, so you're wondering what you're doing in one.

Ironically, I'm starting to take on your former attitude. This weekend, hopping from one church to another was no more than a series of gigs. I wasn't sitting in the pews. I was conducting, playing and singing – doing what I've always done as a musician. I feel a little like Luz at the "Messiah" performance. I'm showing up to perform music, not to have a religious experience.

On Christmas Eve, some of my choir members, knowing our situation, asked if we planned to give our child Christmas gifts next year. I said there was no need since the Hannukah gifts stretch for eight nights.

"But won't you even hang a little stocking for him?"

It's strange. Why do they think that a child raised in one religion will need more?

If our child's personal identity is Jewish, I'm not sure it matters what we do in our professional lives. No one is forcing you to sing in a church. But I'm perfectly happy continuing to perform, whether it happens to be in a church or not.

Love,

Gayle

ॐॐ

February 24, 2000

Dear Gayle,

I'm reading *The Sabbath* by Abraham Joshua Heschel. This is not the Sabbath of my Monroe Temple childhood.

Heschel was a major Jewish philosopher of the 20th century. I only knew of him as the rabbi who mentored and marched with Dr. Martin Luther King. Now I'm discovering the other Heschel.

Heschel speaks of the everyday world as a world of "space" and Shabbat as a world of "time." He calls Shabbat a "palace in time," a structure that attunes us to "holiness in time." Shabbat, he says, calls us to leave the end results of creation and attend to the mystery of creation.

For Heschel, the Torah's laws create the framework of Shabbat, while a person's soul drinks in its spirit. Heschel questions what the world would be like without Shabbat, whether a world that is only space, only things, only the mundane, would be a world worth having. Because Shabbat moves us from space to the realm of time, it opens a window beyond the everyday that transcends both our limited selves and the world we see around us.

Heschel's brilliance aside, I'm beginning to realize that Shabbat holds some practical value. We're always running. Working, shopping, then working again, then shopping again. On a purely psychological level, consciously taking a respite from everything that life sends our way could be just what we need.

Put another way, as we prepare to welcome a child into our lives, I want something more. We could go on like this for decades – advancing in our careers, cutting out the coupons in the sales circulars, running errands, searching for the next good restaurant, taking the occasional vacation or museum visit or concert outing.

I'm not suggesting that that's the sum total of our lives. We follow the news. We get together with friends. We discuss important issues. It's all very nice, but there must be a deeper reason why we're here in the first place.

I'm sorry if I'm not explaining this well. I can't yet articulate this extra something I'm looking for. But somehow, I feel Shabbat may be a key to this elusive whatever-it-is. If, as Heschel says, our regular lives are all about manipulating things in space, then that implies a material existence that is inherently incomplete. The realm of time, on the other hand, suggests a life attuned to what is ultimately important. The cliché is nevertheless true that, at the end of our lives, we don't focus on our house, our car, and all the things we bought in Walmart along the way. We focus on relationships, the events that changed us, our triumphs, our failures – in other words, the things that took place in the realm of time.

At the very least, it would be nice every so often to carve out a retreat from all of life's pressures, relax a little, and get our bearings again before jumping into the fray. I don't want my life to be only about running, running, running all the time.

Last Saturday, I tried a secret experiment. I decided to take a small amount of time that would just be mine, that would acknowledge the day as Shabbat.

My experiment failed. We got in the car to go shopping. As the day wore on, I kept telling myself that there would be time later on. Just one more store. Just one more errand. And before I knew it, you were asking me whether I wanted to go to a restaurant for dinner. All day, I had Shabbat on my mind. But I passively waited for the moment that never came.

I am not complaining. That would be unfair, since I kept the experiment to myself and gave you no chance to opt in or out. Thoreau famously said, "The mass of men lead lives of quiet desperation." I don't want to be like all those people who go through life with their true selves trapped inside as a different existence is thrust upon them. Saturday drove that home.

I want to try Shabbat. It's been two months since I figured out that I don't want to spend Shabbat singing in a church. Now I know that I don't want to spend it in a shopping mall either. I'm not ready to devote an entire day to it, and I can't imagine that you are either. Especially when you have a rehearsal first thing every Saturday morning. Perhaps I can go to services while you're at rehearsal, and then we can take an hour or so and shut off the phone, shut off the TV, shut off the world's distractions – a deliberate time that belongs only to us.

I'm sorry to keep surprising you with my little revelations. But what I'm doing isn't so off the wall. In all the churches where you've worked, it's the norm for congregants to show up most Sundays. Only in Judaism is someone who comes once a month or so considered devout.

We'll still have plenty of Saturday left to do other things. Don't worry. I'm not going off the deep end. But I am thinking deeply about what my life should stand for and what it should look like.

Love,

Harold

March 1, 2000

Dear Harold,

Yes, Christians do think it's normal to go to church every week, at least once you get beyond the C&E crowd. Jews, less so, I've noticed. If you want to go on Saturday mornings, I promise not to think you've gone off the deep end. We already kind of have our own special time on Friday nights, at least when rehearsals and performances don't pull me away.

What you're describing for Saturday after services sounds a bit more drastic. But carving out a special time just for us does have a certain appeal. I don't know how practical it is, though, given all the demands on our time.

I still think some of what drives your search is our soon-to-be-parents status. Not that you are thinking seriously about Judaism only because a child is entering the picture; just that, so I'm told, children are often a wake-up call to look at the future differently.

You're not the only one who's been thinking about the future. All those years when being a parent applied to someone else. All these months of waiting, filling out forms, then waiting again. And anytime now, the phone will ring, and everything will change. Not a little bit – completely.

When I am at home, I imagine a little one running around these until-now quiet rooms. When I am at work, I wonder where our son will be and in whose hands I will feel comfortable leaving him. When I am at church, I worry about how our little one will come to know that place as "Mommy's work" and if it will be confusing to see Mommy at church while the family goes to temple together.

When I'm at Temple Shalom on Friday nights, I try to envision him toddling around the service. And I wonder if there will be anyone for him to befriend. It seems most families take their children to that one Friday night a month when there's a Shabbat dinner. And from what I gather, Saturday morning attracts more people eligible for AARP membership than it does children.

Still, Temple Shalom has turned out to be a great place for a family like ours. At the last temple Shabbat dinner, I started to break into a cold sweat when the man across the table said, "So, Gayle, you're a musician. What kind of music do you perform? Where do you work?" I teetered between spilling the beans that I'm a church organist, and quickly mumbling that I teach piano and voice while politely changing the subject.

But I'm who I am. I have nothing to hide. Still, when I looked him in the eye and said I'm the Music Director and Organist at United Church in Walpole, I half-expected the room to fall silent and every gaze turn in my direction.

Not only did the conversations around the room continue unabated. The man across the table, it turns out, also is a musician who plays organ in a church. And he's Jewish.

Nor does the congregation seem to mind that I direct the Gilbert & Sullivan Players in Boston on Saturday mornings. Everyone is so welcoming, and so understanding.

Being an interfaith family is going to make for a marathon weekend. On Friday nights, the three of us will go to synagogue. Saturday mornings, you'll return with the heir to the Berman family fortune while I go off to rehearsal. Carving out a special time later on Saturday – to be discussed. And on Sunday mornings, the two of you can have fun together while I "do my thing" at the church.

The phrase "the three of us" still boggles my mind. We need to start getting furniture for the baby's room.

Love,

Gayle

April 6, 2000

Dear Harold,

I knew we should have bought the baby furniture sooner. For months, I've imagined the phone ringing, and the voice on the other end telling us to get our plane tickets to Russia. But I never imagined they'd tell us we had to be there by next week!

Nor that we would have to travel the first day of Spring Break when every flight is booked (the travel agent said she's working on it). Nor that I would need to miss both Palm Sunday and Easter. It's like the Cantor telling Temple Shalom in early September that, by the way, he won't be there after all for Rosh Hashanah and Yom Kippur.

Fortunately, everyone at the church understands the big picture here. Unfortunately, finding a substitute organist who is still available for both Palm Sunday and Easter is even more difficult than finding a flight out during Spring Break. I must have called every organist in Massachusetts.

Wait – the phone is ringing. I'd better get it. It's probably the travel agent . . .

Like you often say, things have a way of working out. An organist who couldn't substitute for me called a friend, who called a friend, who called a friend. And she can do it! She said she had to say yes because thirty years ago, someone filled in for her when she adopted her son.

All we need now are plane tickets, and then it's time to pack. We need to get baby clothes. And toys. And the camera. Our passports. And all those documents. And a million other things. Oh, and a box of matzah. Do you realize that, in addition to Easter, we'll be there during Passover?

Love,

Gayle

☙❧

May 10, 2000

Dear Gayle,

Micah Alexander Berman. Sometimes I say the name to myself over and over, letting it roll off the tongue, letting it sink in that we are living a miracle. Four weeks ago, we were a couple. Today, we're a family. Just four weeks, a journey of 4,500 miles – and light years from our former selves.

The space in between plays now and again in my mind like a movie, or perhaps more like a dream. In the real world, I watch Micah playing with his blocks. And it seems like it's always been that way. Like we never got on that plane. Like Murmansk Baby Home No. 1 never existed.

The photos anchor me – we were there. It all happened. There's Dmitri, our driver, always concerned that Micah's wearing enough for the Murmansk winter that extends well into the spring. There's Marina, our adoption facilitator, wearing her trademark electric blue coat. There's Murmansk's grim Soviet architecture, framed by April snow and an Arctic sky.

There we are in Murmansk Baby Home No. 1. Dedicated, but overworked, caretakers trying to attend to over a dozen babies at a time. Children rocking themselves back and forth just to feel some sense of stimulation in the absence of a loving parent's arms. Stark steel cribs crowded together in a room where one-year-olds fall asleep without a mother's goodnight kiss. Those tiny, expectant eyes looking up at us from every corner. The two of us walking out the door with Micah, knowing that most of them will know no other childhood than this.

The scene unfolds again in my mind as Micah sits on our kitchen floor, making fast work of the blocks. I wonder, for what must be the fiftieth time, if I'm worthy to be this child's father. If I can be the role model he needs me to be. If I'll be deserving of his trust, of his love.

I marvel too that you and I are raising a Jewish child. You, who grew up Presbyterian and have worked in a church forever. I, who grew up a Reform Jew who all these years never did much Jewish myself, never mind imparting it to a child.

This child, in particular, may or may not have Jewish ancestry. We'll never know. But we do know that, were he not in our family, he would not be raised as a Jew. When two Jews have a child biologically, raising him as a Jew is a no-brainer. There's no struggle, no discussions of compromise, no concerns about sending mixed messages. But adopting and then converting a child makes taking the Jewish part for granted nearly impossible.

Why are we doing this? It's a question we must ask. I've decided Judaism is a gift, one that I've only recently begun to unwrap, but that is well worth passing on to this child of ours.

The questions fade. It was all meant to be. I can't prove it. I just know it, down to my very core.

Love,

Harold

❧

May 11, 2000

Dear Harold,

I don't need the photos. In my mind, it's all so real, as if we're still there. I smile when I think of laying eyes on this adorable little boy for the first time. I was in heaven when he called out, "Momma, Papa," as we walked in on his toddler music class. I thought, "He's a genius!" when he seemed to know everything the music teacher asked. I guess that's how mothers think about their children.

Beyond the orphanage, the memory that stays with me the most is the court hearing. I started to get nervous when the judge grilled the social worker about the birth parents. And then, just before the judge focused her gaze on me, I felt a very definite chill in the air.

I turned to Marina – "What is she asking me?"

"She noticed in your papers that you said you will be raising him Jewish. She wants to know about that." Big, deep breath. A few sentences later, I thought it was over. But then the judge wouldn't let it go.

"She wants to know if you will be circumcising the child. How will you do it? In a hospital?"

Yes, in a hospital.

Why was she interrogating me? Shouldn't she have asked you? Here I am, the Christian in the family, telling the judge that yes, despite the orphanage director's scowl of disapproval, we are going to raise this child as a Jew. No, don't worry – it will all be done in a hospital. Completely safe. Big, deep breath.

I think you owe me.

After the emotional roller coaster of Murmansk, I needed those few days in Moscow before returning home. I think we were the only non-Russians on the Murmansk to Moscow flight. We certainly were the only ones asking the flight attendant for coffee instead of vodka at 7:30 in the morning.

I still chuckle when I think about our visit to the Russian Orthodox cathedral during our Moscow tour. As we ascended the many steps outside the mammoth church, I saw the guide put a scarf on her head and asked if I should do the same out of respect. When she replied, "Are you Orthodox?," I thought, "Not in either religion," but held my tongue.

So what does it mean that we're raising Micah as a Jew, now that I've defended our decision before the court? In addition to temple and Hebrew school, I know it means a circumcision. I'm pretty nervous even thinking about it. But after all, I also defended that before the court.

May I remind you that I was the one who first suggested we raise him Jewish. I can't tell you why. But I agree – it seems like it was all meant to be.

In the meantime, I love being his mother beyond anything I could ever have imagined.

Love,

Gayle

༜ ༜

June 8, 2000

Dear Harold,

I am barely on speaking terms with God. The Creator of the Universe, the One who is supposed to be compassionate and loving, actually requires this atrocity to be foisted on this unsuspecting baby?

Judaism says that this barbarity connects Micah to God. How? All I see is pain. All I see is Micah's trusting eyes just before he went under and they carted him into surgery. I betrayed that trust. He didn't need this. There was nothing wrong with him.

Maybe it's no big deal for an eight-day old baby to go under the knife. It's all over in a less than a minute. But it's three days later, and this fifteen-month old boy is still in agony.

The only comic relief, if you can call it that, was doing the circumcision in a Catholic hospital. It's not every day you get to see a Catholic nurse ask a Jewish doctor, "What are we doing with him today?" and then watch her jaw drop as the doctor matter-of-factly replies, "Today, we're going to make this boy a Jew."

I keep asking God why it takes so much pain to make this boy a Jew. I'm still awaiting His answer.

I managed to forget my anger for one brief moment. As Micah came to, wailing in fear, I held him until he fell into a deep, peaceful sleep. The nurse said, "There's nothing like a mom." At that moment, I knew fully that he's my son and will be forever.

But after three days, he's still wailing every time I try to change the dressing. Over and over, I've yelled at God. How could we have done this to our little boy? The doctor did a check-up today and said it's healing beautifully. I'd sure hate to see what "healing badly" means.

Why God supposedly requires this horrible act as the male admission ticket to the Jewish people, I'll never understand. In Evangelical churches, they do an altar call. You go to the front of the church, profess your faith, and you're done. No surgery required. I imagine if it were, churches would be empty on Sunday mornings.

I only pray that Micah heals quickly and isn't psychologically scarred for life.

Love,

Gayle

ॐ◌

June 9, 2000

Dear Gayle,

I don't know what to say. I watch Micah in pain, and feel just as bad, and just as helpless. And I know it doesn't help to say that he'll feel much better in a week. He's hurting right now.

I don't know why Judaism requires circumcision. I also can't imagine it any other way. Parts of the Torah are easy to understand. It's no great act of faith to believe that we should love our neighbor as ourselves or that we shouldn't steal. Keeping kosher is a bit more of a leap. And circumcision-Brit Milah is the hardest of all. There are various symbolic and even mystical meanings, but I doubt anyone does this to stay current with Jewish mysticism.

I read that Abraham was 99 years old when God commanded him to circumcise himself. And he had to do it to himself, without a mohel, hospital, anesthesia or pain-killers. I can't imagine.

It made no more sense back then. The only difference was that Abraham heard it from God Himself. The Divine Voice would have been rather difficult to ignore. Now we do it because it's in the Torah and Jews have been doing it these thousands of years since Abraham.

Maybe it's meant to be harder than an altar call. Maybe God is saying that, to be Jewish, He doesn't want simply a profession of faith, an act of mind or even of heart, but all of us. And I suppose that a real relationship with God must, by definition, hold nothing back.

In the meantime, I just hope he recovers quickly and this is soon behind us. I've heard people say that being Jewish is a blessing. But I've never heard anyone say it's easy.

Love,

Harold

৵৽

September 30 (Rosh Hashanah), 2000

Dear Harold,

I never thought that a Rosh Hashanah service could feel like a cocktail party. With the spontaneous explosion of conversation following Rabbi

Fogel's sermon, all we needed were a few waitresses to come out with platters, napkins and those toothpicks with the sparklies on the end.

The Cantor did his best to keep going and to act as if it didn't bother him. But I know it did. The conversations overwhelmed the room, and not one that I heard had a thing to do with Rosh Hashanah. I wondered which part of the service we had come to that could be so trivial to merit this roar of chatting over the Cantor's singing.

I looked down at the prayer book, trying to shut out the din and focus on the words. The Hebrew, which I do hope to learn someday, remains a mystery for the time being. So my eyes naturally drifted to the English side of the prayer book – "Hineni – Here I am."

"Here I am, impoverished of deeds, trembling and frightened," so "Hineni" begins.

I wondered at the powerful wording, already a little mysterious. I read on:

"I have come to stand and supplicate before You for Your people Israel, who have sent me, although I am unworthy and unqualified to do so."

Definitely not trivial. This should have been a profound moment of the service. Instead, the congregation was content to let the Cantor stand and supplicate while they continued chatting about their lunch plans. I thought about the class we had taken before the High Holidays, where we learned that on Rosh Hashanah we talk with God about how we're going to improve ourselves during the coming year. We ask for God's help to overcome all obstacles in our path. Or in the words of "Hineni," we ask God to "denounce the Adversary that he not impede me."

By this point, the conversation had swelled to an even higher decibel, as if defying the Cantor's pleas on their behalf. The thought crossed my mind that the congregation had happily become its own adversary. I read the explanation about "Hineni" at the bottom of the page, which said that this breathtaking prayer has been a feature of the Rosh Hashanah service for perhaps 1,000 years. The Cantor fervently pleads on behalf of his congregation. Because of the enormity of the task, he approaches it with trepidation.

I read on:

"May You transform all travail and evil to joy and gladness, to life and peace, for us and for all Israel, who love truth and peace. And may there be no stumbling block in my prayer."

Stumbling block? The Cantor had just sung his heart out, trying mightily to be heard over the full-throated private conversations of several hundred congregants. As I thought about the irony, the tears began to flow.

I was sad for the congregation, who had just traded one of the highlights of Jewish prayer for conversations that easily could have taken place in a bar. Such an awesome moment, and they missed it.

The tears continued. Not only tears of sadness. Anger, too. Lots of it.

Hineni – here I am, trying so hard to raise a Jewish child. Just a few months ago, we put Micah through the pain of circumcision at fifteen months. I'm going with you on Friday nights, even though most of the congregation doesn't bother to show up – that is, except when dinner's being served after the service. We went to the High Holidays class so we could learn about this together, only to discover that all of four other congregants opted to do the same. You're doing more and more to take Shabbat seriously. We're both reading so that we can be prepared to teach Micah. I'm constantly worrying about how my professional work in a church might affect Micah's Jewish identity.

I'm doing all this, and I'm not Jewish. But I go to temple on the second holiest day of the Jewish year, only to find that the Jews around me can't be bothered to shut up for five minutes while the Cantor is praying on their behalf. All of this hard work we're doing, and I'm greeted with everyone shouting the neighborhood gossip over "and may there be no stumbling block in my prayer."

I keep hearing about the Jewish community's concern over intermarriage. How am I supposed to take their concern seriously when so many Jews don't take Judaism seriously?

Love,

Gayle

❧❦

October 11, 2000

Dear Gayle,

I'm beginning to wonder who I am –and where we fit in. We're an interfaith family who, until recently, had sporadic contact with the Jewish community. And we're upset with Jews who don't take Judaism seriously. Perhaps we defy labels.

A couple of weeks ago, I stumbled upon a web site for interfaith families. When I read that the site's mission is to help intermarried families make Jewish choices, I thought I had found the address for families like ours. Only it isn't.

The site is stuffed with articles – articles about the "December Dilemma," the Easter-Passover dilemma, and a few other dilemmas I had not known existed. Dilemmas that somehow haven't crossed our path much.

It's not only that we solved the "to tree or not to tree" question early on, or that we were in sync when it came time to determine our child's religious identity. It's a difference in mindset.

On the discussion groups, where I've been spending too much of my time, each comment is like a brick in a sky-high wall of rationalization. One parent insists that practicing two religions inside the home won't have any negative impact on her children. After all, she claims, her three-year old has yet to show signs of an identity crisis. Another trips over herself to show that a Christmas tree is ok for children who are being raised Jewish because it doesn't really have anything to do with Christmas – yeah, I guess that's why they call it a *Christmas* tree.

But it's not all chuckles among the interfaith chatters. An occasional chink in the armor will appear, as a parent admits that being in an interfaith family does offer special challenges after all. But, upon sighting Orthodox Jews, the armor goes back up in record time.

Orthodox Jews – what are they are doing on a web site for the intermarried? I have no idea. But a few Orthodox Jews lurk around the discussions and occasionally point out things the intermarried chatters don't like to hear. Like there may be some differences between a Jewish family and an interfaith family. Or that a child not born of a Jewish mother and not converted may not fit the definition of Jewish that has been used for a few thousand years. Or that raising a child with Christmas trees, Easter eggs and the occasional church service may not be the most sure-fire method of fostering a strong Jewish identity.

When the Orthodox dare to intrude, everyone races to condemn them as close-minded, intolerant Neanderthals. Following the condemnation, more bricks are laid in the rationalization wall. We hear that interfaith marriage actually is better for the child, because after all, we live in a multi-cultural society and raising a child with more than one religion will teach him how to be tolerant. If this is true, then they should also be raising their children with Hinduism, Islam, Buddhism and Scientology. If two religions are good, surely six are fantastic.

So here's my dilemma – I'm intermarried, but as I follow these conversations, I find myself siding with the Orthodox. Many of their points make sense, and are grounded in knowledge. Much of what the intermarrieds say strikes me as so much cover for their "neither of us can compromise on our religions for the sake of the children" reality. One woman, married to a Catholic, relates with pride that her children call themselves "Ca-Jews." This way, neither she nor her husband feel left out, even if the kids may have trouble finding a Ca-Jew congregation when they grow up.

And something else bothers me. Even as many of the intermarried are busy condemning the Orthodox for their intolerance, it is the intermarried that seem unwilling to consider viewpoints far from their own. I suppose "intolerant" is a good word to throw at someone if you don't have a better response.

Not only do I find myself siding with the Orthodox. When I posted something, everyone assumed I was Orthodox and labeled me a fanatic too. When I pointed out that I am intermarried, they labeled me an intermarried fanatic.

Each time I go to this site, I feel a kind of religious vertigo. I can't be the only Jew in an intermarriage who doesn't want to rationalize away my life choices. And you can't be the only non-Jew in an intermarriage who wants something more than Judaism-lite made available at your convenience.

Where do we fit in? Not with the two-religions-is-better-than-one crowd. Not with the crowd who gives their kids just enough to get through the Bar Mitzvah, but not a bit more lest it interfere with the important things in life. Like Saturday morning soccer games.

The obvious answer would be to search out a more traditional corner of the Jewish community. But that doesn't work either. One of us plays organ and conducts a church choir, while the other has sung in far more churches than synagogues, yet is annoyed by the messages on an interfaith web site.

I did strike up a conversation with one of the Orthodox Jews on the site, even continuing off-line. His name is Phil Silverman. He's what they call a Baal Teshuvah, someone who grew up with little Jewish education or observance, but nevertheless swam against the tide to become Orthodox. It turns out there are tens of thousands of them out there. Despite all the stereotypes, he doesn't sound like much of a fanatic, just a bright, level-headed person who is trying to be the best Jew he can. I've noticed he accepts nothing blindly, and in fact is far more willing to look at all sides of an issue than are most of the chatters on the web site.

Phil suggested I look up Aish HaTorah, an organization that hosts classes and events for people who want to learn more about Judaism. Aish, as people call it, is Orthodox, which still is like a foreign country to me (at least when I'm not on an intermarried web site). But according to Phil, they are non-judgmental and teach everyone.

I may look into it. I'm not sure yet. Can we be the only ones in this boat?

Love,

Harold

෨෬

October 17, 2000

Dear Harold,

The mikveh was much easier than the circumcision! I woke up this morning rehearsing what we would say to the rabbis, how we would convince them that this interfaith couple is sincere in their decision to raise Micah as a Jew. Now that it's over, I have no idea what they thought, since they never bothered to call us into the room. I don't know what Rabbi Fogel said to them, although any time I walked by, all I heard was small talk coming through the half-open door. Strange that they didn't feel the need to speak with the parents of the little convert before the big dunk.

They were nice to let me stand in the mikveh room and watch. They even said I could take pictures. Since I couldn't take Micah in myself, not being Jewish, this gave me a way to feel a part of things. Even though you managed to dunk him without drowning him, Micah sounded like he was going through the circumcision again. God may have had some trouble hearing the rabbis say the blessings over the weeping and wailing.

I certainly had trouble hearing them. I'm not sure why the rabbis never entered the mikveh room, remaining unseeing and unseen from the adjoining room. Who were the other two rabbis, anyway? I understood that they were from two other Conservative temples, but they introduced themselves so quickly that I didn't catch their names.

I wonder if Micah feels any different now. The circumcision became momentous for me, if only because of the pain. I expected the mikveh to feel momentous too. It was special, just the three of us in the room together (and it's very clear to me where the idea of baptism came from). But I had expected more from the rabbis.

I hadn't envisioned that they wouldn't even be interested in speaking with us beforehand, they wouldn't be interested in witnessing the event as it was happening, and they wouldn't show any more enthusiasm than a half-hearted "mazel tov" at the end before they scurried away. We walked outside, and I wondered, "Is that it? Is it over?"

Micah certainly looks happy. Although swimming lessons are next on the "to do" list.

I guess I'm the minority in our family now.

Love,

Gayle

৵৩

Dear Gayle,

Ever since finding that interfaith web site, I'm seeing things differently. For years, I reflexively nodded my head when people ranted about how the Orthodox are intolerant. Now, I'm starting to see the deep prejudices many people who consider themselves open-minded have against the Orthodox. No doubt, some is driven by personal experience. But there's a visceral dislike that can't be explained away so easily.

I see this on the web site. Some of the Orthodox who post on the discussion boards have, shall we say, a less than diplomatic way of airing their views. But this is met with an explosion of anger that's massively disproportionate. Even when someone like Phil Silverman states his views as politely as possible, the explosion flares just the same.

These anti-Orthodox polemics exist not only in cyberspace, but in real life. At Temple Shalom, I'll overhear an offhand comment, a joke, a stereotype – all stated as scientific fact. The remarks seem innocent enough – except that, more often than not, if you were to substitute "African-American," "Hispanic," etc. where they say "Orthodox," it would no longer sound innocent.

On Saturday mornings, I'm hearing about the Orthodox from the pulpit. Perhaps Rabbi Fogel had a bad experience that he's acting out in his sermons. Whatever the reason, somewhere in his message is a reminder that the Orthodox are not our friends. Whether the theme is Abraham finding God, Moses at the burning bush, or the rites of the priests in the ancient Temple, it all somehow finds its way back to the Orthodox.

Last week, it found its way back to Joe Lieberman. As the first Jewish Vice Presidential candidate in history, the media have covered Lieberman's Orthodox practices extensively in the context of his political life. I've been intrigued by how he's gained the respect of his peers – who call him "the moral conscience of the Senate" – because of how he lives his life. After hearing so many Jews speak of Jewish observance as something that restricts you, I've been amazed to watch how Lieberman incorporates it into his very high-profile role. He's advanced to where he is and become who he is, not despite his Jewish observance, but because of it.

Rabbi Fogel spoke about all of this, making a case for the power of Jewish values. So far, so good. But then, we inevitably made our way back to the Orthodox. We heard that Joe Lieberman isn't really an Orthodox Jew. Yes, it's true – he calls himself an Orthodox Jew and he attends an Orthodox synagogue. But the sterling Jewish values he displays aren't really Orthodox. In fact, Joe Lieberman isn't Orthodox at all. He's a very observant Conservative Jew.

I almost laughed aloud. Then I wondered why is this rabbi investing so much in the idea that there's nothing good about the Orthodox, even to the point of relabeling a good Orthodox Jew as Conservative?

There's a third rail buried underneath all the comments and stereotypes and rationalizations. I think I'll go to a class at Aish after all. I couldn't imagine being Orthodox. But I want to see what all the fuss is about.

Love,

Harold

৵৵

October 30, 2000

Dear Harold,

It's very strange. As a Christian married to a Jew, I keep bumping into converts at every turn. The other day, I was speaking with Robert at Temple Shalom. I was curious why Robert became Jewish since he had been active in the temple for many years without converting.

What, I asked him, led him to convert? Everyone at Temple Shalom is so welcoming and inclusive, and they make it easy for people who aren't Jewish to feel a part of the congregation.

Without hesitating, he said, "How could I ask my children to do something I was unwilling to do myself?" It's hard to find fault with his reasoning. Or with his commitment. He's on the Board, reads from the Torah, and is more active than most members of the congregation.

It may not be so unusual to cross paths with a convert at Temple Shalom. But recently, I was speaking with our neighbor, Melissa, who casually mentioned a friend of hers who used to live a few blocks away. The friend was not born Jewish, but her husband was. They also went to Temple Shalom. Eventually, she converted and they decided they wanted to live in a stronger Jewish community. Melissa's description made me curious, so I called her friend to find out more. She told me that, over time, they began taking on more and more of the Jewish way of life. They started to "play" at keeping kosher and wanted to walk to synagogue on Shabbat. Ultimately, they moved to Lexington where the Jewish community is much larger and they could feel a part of things rather than sticking out like sore thumbs for being observant.

And then there's my "other life" at United Church in Walpole. This was supposed to be a one-year interim position, since I didn't know if I would be able to juggle all of the responsibilities once I became a mother. I'm still there for a few reasons. John Lilly has to be the nicest and most knowledgeable pastor a church musician could hope for. I love playing the Casavant pipe organ. And I love directing the choirs, which are filled with genuinely great people who work hard and make some beautiful music.

But even at United Church, living a committed Jewish life has come up. At my last choir rehearsal, one of the members started talking about a friend of hers who is an Orthodox Jew. They spent a few days together recently, and the choir member went on and on about how her friend's house is so full of warmth and love for God. She did observe one thing that confused her. The wife always covers her hair, supposedly so that she won't be attractive to any man other than her husband. Yet, when she gets dressed up, she wears a wig that makes her drop dead gorgeous. So how does this make her less attractive to other men? I suppose no one can be consistent 100% of the time.

Back to Temple Shalom. As we were sitting around after the last Tot Shabbat service with our apples and juice, Rabbi Fogel noticed that all four of the children who came were adopted and had been born in four different countries. I loved that we had an international tot congregation, but isn't it a shame that only four parents bothered to bring their children? Where were all the other families, whose children were born in the U.S.? I don't think it was an accident that all of the children were adopted. We had to make a conscious decision that our children would be Jewish, so we don't take it for granted. But the born Jewish children are going to start taking it for granted before long, if that's what their parents do.

Since the Tot Shabbat service fell right around the High Holidays, Rabbi Fogel brought out a shofar for the children to try. He couldn't have known that Micah had been experimenting on my old bugle, and was blown away when Micah started getting a real sound out of the shofar. When my turn came, the sounds came pretty easily, no doubt a holdover from my trumpet-playing days.

As I finished, Rabbi Fogel laughed and said, "Now we just need to go to the mikveh to make it official." Am I missing something here? I really am not thinking about converting, yet it's following me everywhere I go. I do think that it's important to take the religion seriously if you're raising a child in it, but that doesn't automatically make me a candidate for conversion.

Beyond Temple Shalom and United Church, there are my Evangelical students at Eastern Nazarene College, my students (many of whom are Jewish) at the Boston Music Center on Saturday mornings, and my professional performing. I do have an interesting view perched on this fence overlooking Christianity and Judaism.

Love,

Gayle

November 9, 2000

Dear Gayle,

"We wrote it."

"Yes. Exactly."

We wrote it? We?

The evening began innocently – a small group of temple members gathering at Michael's home to learn Torah with a gifted rabbi. Far more promising than hearing the Cantor talked over during *Hineni* or coming to services where you not only have your choice of seats, but of entire rows.

I could overlook the rabbi's a-bit-too-studied mannerisms, or his penetrating look as someone stated the obvious. Amidst the histrionics, he offered insights I had never heard before. He made connections between parts of the text that were so nuanced, yet so real, that I began to understand in a new way just how deep the Torah is. There's so much there that defies a superficial reading. And even the most rudimentary understanding of Hebrew yields meanings that are impenetrable in translation. I was starting to realize why the Torah has sustained the Jews for thousands of years through every conceivable situation.

My reverie abruptly ended as a woman began to near-shout from across the room. She was all worked up about the static (to her) nature of the prayers and her awkward relationship to Jewish ritual. Only, her rant had nothing to do with the passages in Genesis we were studying. To my surprise, the rabbi just nodded with his signature penetrating look.

Others seemed only too happy to join in, more interested in projecting their issues onto Judaism than learning how Judaism might speak to their issues. Just as I began to feel I was at a group therapy session, the rabbi managed to steer the conversation back to Genesis.

And then, out of the blue, the husband of the ranting woman sat back smugly and proclaimed, "We wrote it." Meaning – we wrote the Torah. To which the rabbi responded, "Exactly."

I thought to myself, we've just learned about some incredibly complex and beautiful meanings under the surface of the text. We've just uncovered a level of subtlety that should be well beyond the grasp of "primitive" people from Biblical times. And all this guy can say is, "We wrote it." Even if one decided that the Torah was written 100% by dead white men, still, "we" didn't write anything. "We" only inherited the text.

Driving home, I resolved that I would finally try Aish this week. So I showed up for their weekly Torah class on Wednesday. Like night and day. About 50 people filled the room. I was told that sometimes as many as 75 come, all by word of mouth.

Rabbi Glaser, the Aish Rabbi, is more interested in teaching the Torah than in giving penetrating looks. And the people who come there are searching and questioning. Rabbi Glaser encourages all questions. He doesn't expect people to take what he says on blind faith. He expects questions. He expects skepticism. He even welcomes it.

Growing up, I had always thought of Orthodox Jews as being closed to questions. You leave your thinking self at the door, you follow the rules, and that's that.

And yet – that's not at all what I experienced. Nor, apparently did the others in the class. During the break, I spoke with a young woman whose parents are intermarried. She grew up barely knowing she was Jewish, and has only recently come to it. As I talked about how the kids in my temple growing up didn't learn Torah like this, and most left after Bar Mitzvah, she pointed to the Bible on the table and said, "I don't understand how you can take *this*, and make it boring." I'm beginning to wonder, too.

Rabbi Glaser introduced himself at the end. I decided to be honest about who we are. He was equally honest about Judaism's view of intermarriage. I would have been offended, except that he said it respectfully, and at the same time made clear that I had a place there. More than that – as I left, he said, "Please tell Gayle she's welcome anytime."

I'm starting to feel like I'm swimming between two poles, but I'm not sure what this area is in the middle – or if I'll need a life vest out here.

Love,

Harold

ॐॐ

November 17, 2000

Dear Harold,

Now that we're past the circumcision and the mikveh, Micah feels right at home with Judaism, sometimes in ways that are awkward in my situation. I thought it would be safe to ask students from Eastern Nazarene College to babysit while I teach. But when I went to get him last week, the babysitter looked confused. She said he kept touching the top of his head and saying, "Beepah! Beepah!"

"What's a beepah?" she asked. I made up something about his pronunciation of "cap" not being good, and toddlers coming up with all sorts of funny names for things. I couldn't imagine myself standing in the middle of this Evangelical Christian school and saying, "Micah's Jewish, and he wants to wear his kippah, just like he does in temple. A kippah, also known as a yarmulke, is the round cap Jews wear on their heads while praying."

No, I decided not to go down that road with students who believe that anyone who is not a born-again Christian runs the danger of their soul being condemned to eternal damnation.

Just as I started to think that maybe it's time to find a different place for Micah while I'm teaching, the babysitter's friend ran in frantically with Micah in tow. She had been with him in the dorm hallway when her phone rang. As she ran to get it, Micah went running after her. He tripped, and his head flew into the doorpost, leaving a nasty-looking cut on his forehead. I rushed him to the pediatrician – fortunately, everything's ok.

The babysitter is now wondering if a college dorm is a safe place for toddlers. She's probably right, and with the Jewish element, she's more right than she realizes.

What to do with him while I'm teaching – any ideas?

Love,

Gayle

ॐ๛

December 11, 2000

Dear Gayle,

They've asked me to join the Rabbinic Search Committee, to co-chair it no less. A bit of a surprise, since we've been at Temple Shalom for barely a year. I said yes immediately. Between the empty seats on Saturday mornings, and feeling pulled away by the Aish classes, I thought this might be the ticket to finding my place at Temple Shalom.

I hope it gets better. We've had only one meeting so far, but I left wanting to run to Aish, if for no other reason than I know what they stand for.

The Committee cannot decide what the temple wants to be when it grows up. We are seriously considering resumes from a Reform rabbi, a Reconstructionist rabbi, a Conservative rabbi, a very traditional Conservative rabbi who started out Orthodox, and a few rabbis not affiliated with any movement. Except for Chabad, we've got the spectrum covered.

I humbly suggested to the Committee that the unusually wide range of candidates might possibly suggest a certain lack of clarity on our part. Perhaps we should decide what it is we want and invite only those candidates who fit within our rabbinic vision.

Obviously, I have misunderstood my fellow Committee members. I have mistaken their sense of open inquiry for a lack of clarity, their enthusiasm to scour the entire Jewish world to find just the right candidate for mere confusion. Or so it was explained to me.

Perhaps I am the one who is confused. As I now understand, the Committee is looking for a rabbi who is traditional, but not too traditional. Who is erudite, but down-to-earth. Serious, but with a sense of humor. Who will engage the older members of our congregation, but appeal to the young people. Who knows how to run a traditional Conservative service, but can be "creative" by playing the guitar or making the service shorter. Who has firm convictions, but is flexible. Who is charismatic, but isn't always the center of attention. Who is attuned to synagogue politics, but stays above them.

I don't think they are looking for a rabbi. They are looking for the Messiah.

Love,

Harold

৵৹৵

January 12, 2001

Dear Harold,

I survived my first Orthodox Shabbat dinner. You, too. I couldn't believe how many people Rabbi Glaser and his wife, Zakah, had at their table.

Everything about them is impressive. I was impressed with how Rabbi Glaser related to each person, from those who are observant to those who aren't, to those of us who are not Jewish. I was impressed with how Zakah had cooked so much food. I was especially impressed with how they handled their children. Even when all of that soda landed in a puddle on the white carpet, they kept their cool while the children calmly cleaned it up.

I managed to speak with Zakah alone for a few minutes. She is also a singer, and it sounds like being a singer and a religious Jew at the same time is challenging. Some religious women don't sing in front of men, which limits performing opportunities a bit. She does recording sessions, but I wonder how someone who had a performing career can be satisfied singing in a sound booth.

On top of that, with no performing on Shabbat, a performing career would be all but impossible for a religious Jewish woman. I'm having a hard time reconciling how the warmth of the evening enveloped us with the idea that Judaism could be so limiting.

Love,

Gayle

જી⟡⟍

February 6, 2001

Dear Gayle,

"Make it Bacon!" The words screamed at me. I'm not prepared to say it was a message from God. But coincidence or not, it was hard to ignore.

For the past few months, I had felt perfectly comfortable eating in non-kosher restaurants and simply avoiding meat. But recently, I've had second thoughts. Each time I walk into a restaurant and order my veggie-whatever, this nagging voice in the back of my head starts wondering how it was cooked and what it was cooked with. The Voice has begun to question whether I really know what I'm eating.

As I left work tonight, my nose told my empty stomach that my feet were passing by a McDonalds. With the golden arches coming into view, I noticed my feet turning and my hand pulling the door handle. And then my eyes gazed upon a list of items for only 99 cents. French fries, I thought. That will do me until dinner. It's just potatoes.

The Voice sensed an opening. "Yes, but what do they fry them in?" "Don't worry, it's just vegetable oil," I said. "Vegetable oil that was probably used for the Chicken McNuggets. Didn't you read something about McDonalds using animal fat and not telling people?" "It'll be fine," I assured the Voice. "We're talking about potatoes. And I'm very hungry."

As I wavered, I looked up, and there it was – huge letters on a huge banner all leading toward an exclamation point. "Look around you," the Voice said, sensing victory. "This isn't the Western Wall. This is McDonalds. Cheeseburgers in every corner. And those Egg McMuffins with the ham and sausage. You're telling me that this is really kosher?" "Yes," the Voice insisted in triumph, "you may as well 'Make it Bacon!'"

I had to admit that the Voice had a point. But the thought of eating only in kosher restaurants . . . There are five in Boston, and only two serve edible food.

It's strange, this kosher thing. I can't explain it. I've taken one little step at a time – first no shellfish, then non-kosher meat only when eating out, then only eating vegetarian at restaurants.

Shabbat is rational, beyond whatever religious significance it may have. It's a day of rest, a time to recharge and reflect.

But keeping kosher – I can't explain why I've changed my eating habits at all. There are some beautiful explanations of patterns contained in the Torah's kosher laws. In the Garden of Eden, God tells Adam and Eve that they are free to eat from every tree, except of course for one. There is no killing in the Garden of Eden. Adam and Eve are vegetarians.

The first time an animal is killed is after they eat from the infamous tree, when the Torah says that God makes clothes for Adam and Eve from animal skins. Later, when Noah steps off the ark, God tells him that he may eat "every creature."

The kosher laws are a compromise between these two extremes and hearken back to an almost Eden-like state. There is still killing, but within very narrow parameters. Every animal that is permitted is one that doesn't kill other animals for food. No bird of prey is kosher. In other words, the Torah only permits us to eat animals who are themselves vegetarians. According to Rabbi Kook, the first Chief Rabbi of Israel, the need to eat animals represents a lower spiritual state, and in the time of the Messiah, we will again be vegetarians.

Thus, the laws of kashrut are designed to instill a reverence for life. I read that even the Torah's obligation to separate milk and meat reflects this idea, as milk is the symbol of life, meat is the symbol of death, and the two should not be mixed.

So if it is true that you are what you eat, then keeping kosher makes us more human. Rather than eating simply to fill our stomachs as animals do, every bite I take becomes a spiritual affirmation.

It sounds nice. But I came across these ideas after I started taking steps toward keeping kosher. I've taken each step because of a vague sense that it's what I should do. When I turned tail in the face of "Make it Bacon!" there were no thoughts of affirming life or entering a higher spiritual consciousness. It was simply a persistent feeling that I'm supposed to do this. Because I'm Jewish.

Love,

Harold

ॐॐ

March 4, 2001

Dear Gayle,

I did it. I feel like I crossed some imaginary line in the sand. I went to an Orthodox service and I lived to tell about it.

As I walked toward the synagogue, every pair of eyes was staring at me, or so it seemed. I know it was only me wondering what I was doing there. Still, every innocent glance felt like a dagger.

As I approached the entrance, a different world beckoned. Families walking together. Women chatting amiably as they pushed strollers. Children playing everywhere. The whole scene held a feeling of peace. Not peace, exactly, but a feeling that everything was right, that this is how things are supposed to be. Everyone carried themselves like they belonged, like they were comfortable there, like it was their home.

I felt my heart pounding ever-louder as I approached the door. Each step past another Orthodox Jew brought a fresh wave of anxiety. Every seven-year old in my path whose Jewish knowledge likely surpassed my own sent a new message from my mind to my body: "Run! It's not too late. You don't have to do this. You don't have to make a complete fool of yourself."

I almost did an about-face back to my spiritual comfort zone, except that the time for that had already passed. There was a reason I wasn't at the mall this morning. There was a reason I had stepped off that sleepy path trod by so many – the path that takes you to synagogue for the High Holidays and maybe a Shabbat service here and there when the mood strikes you. The path that teaches your child about six months worth of material in six years of Hebrew school while you focus on other things. The path where Judaism is very important – as long it doesn't get in the way of . . . virtually anything else.

As I edge toward the synagogue, I realize I am not on that path anymore. I don't know what path I'm on now, or if it's a path at all. It could be the edge of a cliff.

I am just ten feet from the door. I have broken out in a cold sweat. Someone is going to discover me. Someone is going to figure out that I don't know anything. Then, someone is going to figure out that I'm intermarried. Someone is going to tell me that I don't belong here. It's not too late to turn back.

I look up. Young Israel of Brookline – etched in stone over a double set of double doors.

I cross the threshold. It's really not so bad, well not yet. People say, "Good Shabbos." It seems like they mean it. The sanctuary is to the right. There is the tallis rack, a familiar jumble of blue and black and white. There are the prayer books, thankfully with an English translation. Maybe this isn't so hard. Maybe the barriers are all in my head.

Open the door to the sanctuary. Walk through it. Take this step by step. Just as things begin to feel normal . . .

Hundreds and hundreds of Jews – a whole sea of them. I ask someone if there is a Bar Mitzvah. No. Perhaps there is some Jewish holiday I don't know about. I've never seen so many Jews in synagogue on a regular Shabbat. It cannot be that they all do this every Saturday.

Once I overcome my shock at the overflow crowd, I am secretly relieved. I can stay anonymous here. No one will know that I don't know the prayers so well. No one will know anything. I can just sit back and observe, and try to follow what's going on.

"Good Shabbos. Are you new in town?" My heart starts to pound again. "Do you have a place for Shabbos lunch?" I assure him that I am all set, as I break into another cold sweat.

Once I get over this intruder nearly blowing my cover, I marvel at what just occurred. Here I am, a complete stranger, and he's inviting me into his home to share a meal with him. This never happened in any temple I've been to before. Must be a special case. There's an overly friendly one in every crowd.

Then come the announcements at the end of the service. "If there are any visitors who need a place to go for Shabbos lunch, please come up front after the service. We have many families who want to host guests." Very strange.

Thankful to preserve my anonymity intact, I opt out of the Kiddush and head for the door. I review the past two hours in my mind. A sea of hundreds of kippah-covered heads. What appears to be a full house of women sitting separately up in the balcony. Not that I could see up there so well – but I guess that's the point. Hundreds of voices singing confidently together. Lots of warmth. Lots of praying like it matters.

It's all so strange – and yet it feels right. Maybe I'll try it again next week.

Love,

Harold

ॐ∙ॐ

March 5, 2001

Dear Harold,

On the one hand, I think you're crazy. Why do you feel this need to eat only kosher? Ok, so it makes you more aware of your food. You can do that without keeping kosher. Surely God gives special dispensation when kosher food is hard to come by and is so much more expensive.

You've been making a lot of other changes lately that are difficult, especially when you tell me after the fact. I don't see why you can't ride in a car to temple. I'm sure God would rather that you get to synagogue safely than put yourself in harm's way during the three-mile walk in the middle of a thunderstorm or blizzard.

On the other hand, I think a lot of other Jews are crazy. I can't stand to see a parent do the minimum for the child to get through a Bar or Bat Mitzvah, with even that minimum ending immediately after the party, only to resume a generation later when the grandchild starts the whole charade again. I can't stand to hear an intermarried parent say, "We're exposing Joey to both religions, and he can decide when he grows up." I've already seen where that goes. I found out that Theresa, my student from Harvard, is the child of an intermarriage who got a bit of both. Many times, she's said, "It would just be nice to know who I am, and where I belong."

On the other hand, I cannot be someone I am not. Since childhood, I have been involved in the life of a church. My place has been to make music in a church. I even make a large part of my living working in a church. Do I give all of that up for the sake of our child's identity with the risk that I might, in the future, come to resent leaving behind a big chunk of my life? Neither of us has ever wanted me to convert "for the sake of the marriage," and I still think it would only cause strife in our family in the end.

On the other hand, what will become of our family if we try to maintain the status quo? You've talked about swimming between two poles, and walking on a path. But you're really on an escalator that is picking up speed and carrying you further and further toward Jewish observance. Micah and I are standing at the foot of the escalator, and you're starting to disappear from view. Do you not love us enough to compromise on your observance? Why did you feel the need to start on this path? Why can't you be happily intermarried like before (or were you?)

On the other hand, Micah loves Judaism in an almost supernatural way. Something deep inside him can't seem to get enough of it. I could never take that away from him. I want him to have all the Jewish education he needs. I still think it was the right choice to raise him as a Jew. I just had no idea it would lead to this. How confusing is it for him when he goes to work with Mommy while she practices organ at the church? When he takes the cushion out of the offering plate and puts it on his head like a kippah? Does he know he's not in a synagogue? Where does he think Mommy's going every Sunday morning, and what will he think of it when he's old enough to understand?

As Tevye said, "On the other hand.......there is no other hand!" I feel lost. I feel helpless. I feel betrayed.

Love,

Gayle

᷐᷌

March 6, 2001

Dear Gayle,

I don't have the answers. You say you have a problem with my increased observance, but you can't stand a minimalist Judaism. Where the middle ground is, I don't know. And unfortunately, our definitions of middle ground are diverging. In truth, we never did have a working definition. We never did spell out what raising a Jewish child, or having a Jewish home in the context of our marriage, would actually look like.

We still do agree, I think, on the general goal. There must be a way to come to terms with the specifics. But I don't see how we can achieve the general goal without the Jewish observance part. Not in a way that doesn't make a sham of the whole thing.

Before last night's Rabbinic Search Committee meeting, I took another glance at Heschel's book about Shabbat. As I pulled into the parking lot and made my way to the synagogue library, Heschel's idea of Shabbat as a "palace in time" was fresh in my mind.

Peter's "Good evening, Harold," broke my Heschel reverie. I asked the perfunctory "How are things going?" expecting a "Fine, and you?"

"Oh, you can't imagine," Peter said, his jaw tense and dark rings circling his eyes. "It's overwhelming. Too much work at work. Fixing the house. The family. This committee. Every time I try to get ahead, I get more behind."

"You know," he said, "wouldn't it be great if someone could invent some mechanism where you could step off the treadmill for a little while, just for a little bit? Even if you had to get back on the treadmill again, you would know that you could get off just long enough to recover yourself. Wouldn't that be great?"

Several of the other committee members nodded their agreement. There I sat, in a library of perhaps 1,000 Jewish books, ten feet from the chapel. I simply nodded along with the others, as I heard Heschel's closing tribute to Shabbat inside my head: "Eternity utters a day."

And with that, we continued reviewing resumes and trying to agree on just what it was we were all looking for in a rabbi.

And that's my dilemma – it doesn't work to talk about Jewish things, or think about Jewish things, or act as if Jewish things are important, without actually doing Jewish things. Shabbat doesn't work if it's not used. Judaism doesn't work with ham sandwiches. Some people do manage to navigate a Judaism without observance and find substitutes that compensate for a time. But Judaism was never designed to work like that.

You had once mentioned that family who used to go to Temple Shalom and moved to Lexington when they became more observant. But they were on the same page.

We're not – although it's still possible we're in different places in the same book. What to do? I don't know. I really don't know.

Love,

Harold

꙳꙳

March 23, 2001

Dear Harold,

Do you remember the morning that sent us on our way to counseling? You made that comment about how you didn't have any clean shirts to wear. I blew up, asking why can't you help around the house, and on top of it, why do I always feel like I am being criticized? Obviously that blow-up was the end result of all the chaos churning under the surface. I just wish you had never become interested in taking on more and more laws.

Today, when I met with the counselor, we discussed my sister Angela marrying Sylvan, a Conservative Jew, and how they both compromised on kosher food in the home. Angela agreed to keep non-kosher food out of the house, and Sylvan agreed that, as long as the food was kosher, he would accept mixing milk and meat. When a Jew marries a non-Jew, I think that a compromise like this makes so much sense. The non-Jew shouldn't be the one who is giving up everything. Any marriage needs to be based on compromise, respect, and giving to the other more than thinking about himself. I don't feel any of that coming from you.

I didn't agree to keep kosher when we got married. I didn't agree to not do anything on Saturdays. I didn't agree to only walk to temple on Shabbat. When you change agreements mid-marriage, you need to be more flexible and considerate. I shouldn't be the only one giving up everything here!

Love,

Gayle

৵৽৽

June 5, 2001

Dear Harold,

Once again, I went along with what you wanted to do – and all I've accomplished is to become more frustrated, hurt and angry. You said we should speak with Rabbi Turtletaub, the Assistant Rabbi at Aish, that you thought he might be able to help us. I went along with it.

And what does he say to me? That if you were to follow all of the mitzvot, you could not stay married to me if I did not accept the same mitzvot and convert Orthodox! Isn't this exactly the kind of mindset we reacted against when we got married?

And where is God in all of this? I haven't been this mad at Him since the circumcision. How can God drive two people apart who have loved each other so much all these years? How can He do this to Micah? Is this the same loving God to Whom I've been praying all these years?

Rabbi Turtletaub recommended we see a specific counselor. She's an Orthodox Jew, of course. This is an ambush. I feel like I've been thrown into the pit like Joseph and have no way out. This is not my fault! Why am I being punished when I've done nothing wrong? How could I even consider converting under these circumstances? How could we have brought Micah into this mess? How could you do this to us?

And each time you add a new observance, you spring it on me without warning. The other night, you watched as I cooked chicken and put milk into the potatoes (as I always do). You stood there and said nothing. Instead, you had to wait until I served the meal to say, "I don't want any potatoes."

And then when Peggy and her husband were here for my birthday, which happened to be on a Saturday, you wouldn't take our picture. You couldn't have said something earlier to save us all from an awkward situation. I bought into your not wanting to pick them up at the airport, but what's the harm in one little snapshot?

The final straw was when your parents were here. I was trying to get the windows washed, having all sorts of problems getting the screens in and out. All you wanted to do was sit and read. I certainly could have used some help! You said that if you didn't work on Shabbat, you'd work that much harder during the week. So far, I haven't seen that happening.

Love failed me once. I'm starting to wonder if I should have trusted it again. How can you not love me enough to compromise on what you feel you need to do as a Jew? There has to be a better way.

I feel abandoned. What are you going to do about this?

Love,

Gayle

❧❧

Dear Gayle,

It's eating me up that I'm causing you so much pain. It's that much worse that I'm hurting you by doing something that's become so meaningful for me.

I don't know what Rabbi Turtletaub said to you in private. I can only tell you what he said to me – that in his time at Aish, he has known several interfaith families where the Jewish spouse became observant. When the non-Jewish spouse was not interested, it made for some rough going. He related to me an incident where the non-Jewish spouse started making fun of the Jewish spouse's new-found observance, and that was the beginning of the end.

The anecdote, unfortunately, relates to us. I understand what I am doing to you, and I am aching over it. At the same time, I feel like you see my Judaism as something whose purpose is to inconvenience you.

I agree that I've been terrible about not telling you in advance where my observance is going. The problem is that I've never gone through this, so I keep trying to figure it out as I go along – usually it seems, to your detriment.

I know that does nothing for you. I don't want to diminish your feelings of hurt one bit – but it's also frustrating for me when I discover something that holds such great meaning, and all it represents to you is another burden.

I'm sorry that I didn't eat the mashed potatoes. I'm sorry that I didn't take the photograph. I'm sorry that I didn't help with the windows. I'm sorry for all of my actions because they caused you pain, which as I said, is the last thing I want to do.

But is my unwillingness to eat your milk potatoes with chicken such an insurmountable issue? Or taking a photograph on Shabbat? Or even helping with the windows (not that I'm so good at that on a weekday)?

Those are not the real issues. Because if they were, then maybe I should feel hurt that, after a decade of marriage, you cannot accept a diet that is far less restrictive than a vegetarian's, or a 25-hour period in which I won't click a camera shutter.

It is the person behind these actions that you find so difficult to accept. This person feels like he is becoming his true self, but his true self is someone you don't recognize as the person you married. I understand that. If I don't know where I am going, then you must be getting dizzy as you try to hold on while I stumble around.

I accept that I am to blame. I am sorry, and I want to find a way to become who I am that doesn't hurt you.

Still, I am sensing something else behind your anger which I find much harder to accept. I didn't even need to sense it, only to listen to your words. When you stormed off after the mashed potato incident, you said, "This is why the Apostle Paul talked about being freed from the law."

This is hardly the time to discuss Paul's grasp of Judaism, or the conflicting ways people understand his words. It is the place, however, to discuss how you understand Judaism.

I have met many Christians, particularly the very liberal ones, who are open-minded about Judaism – but it is the Judaism that they have recast through their Christian lenses. From this liberal viewpoint, Judaism is ok because it is viewed as more or less another Protestant denomination, minus Jesus, and with a bit of Hebrew and a different set of holidays.

That may be convenient for the purposes of interfaith dialogue. But it is not Judaism.

Judaism is ultimately about the law, but not as some Christians have traditionally understood it. The law was given to make our lives more complete, not as a weight around our necks. It is not about mashed potatoes. It is about making holy every single action, no matter how seemingly mundane. For a Jew to live by the law is to discover his innermost self.

And it's not just any old law. Jews have lived and died by it for thousands of years – not as an abstract concept, but as the foundation of their relationship with God, as the very foundation of their lives. For that matter, Jesus also observed Shabbat and kept kosher.

But the law has been unjustly stereotyped over the past 2,000 years. And Paul's words have contributed more than their share to that stereotype. So please permit me to quote something else Paul said: "When I was a child, I used to talk like a child, think like a child, reason like a child. When I became a man, I put away childish things."

When we started going to Beth Am in San Antonio, I met an elderly man there. He had been distant from Judaism for most of his adult life, and had only recently come back to it. I have never forgotten what he said when I asked him what sparked his newfound enthusiasm. "Judaism is an adult religion. I couldn't appreciate it until I had come to a certain place in my life."

At the Monroe Temple of Liberal Judaism, many a Bar Mitzvah had "kosher style" food. By this was meant that the food was cleverly disguised as food that Jews traditionally eat, but in fact was not kosher at all.

I've been living on kosher-style Judaism for too long. I need a Judaism for adults. If not, then I don't see the point of doing it at all.

I know that may sound grim in terms of our future – and it doesn't lessen your pain. Before we jump to any dire conclusions, I want to go back to what I think Rabbi Turtletaub really meant.

After Rabbi Turtletaub described to me the high hurdles we would create if I became observant and you remained Christian, I said he wasn't giving us much hope. To my surprise, he said I shouldn't give up hope at all. That after meeting you, he sensed something. And that, as the Jewish sages say, everything can change "in the blink of an eye." And yes, he also suggested the Orthodox therapist.

I understand your feeling ambushed – if the therapist is Orthodox, then why wouldn't she take my side against yours? May I suggest he gave us the name of this therapist for a reason. If he thought there was no hope, he wouldn't be sending us to a therapist. If he thought there was no hope, he wouldn't be telling us, in effect, to keep trying.

As for her Orthodoxy, Rabbi Turtletaub said he was recommending her specifically because she would understand the issues at stake. We already did the rounds with a secular therapist, who in record time showed that he didn't have a clue about anything we said.

Perhaps we can try. Perhaps we can make an appointment, and keep talking and talking until we know where we really are.

Love,

Harold

෨෧

June 14, 2001

Dear Harold,

OK, I'll try. But I don't mind telling you that it's me who will feel like she's on the hot seat going to this therapist. I can't imagine how a woman who is Orthodox, and married to an Orthodox rabbi no less, can pretend to be objective about our situation. I can't imagine how she would be happy if the result she achieves is to keep an intermarriage intact.

You think the issues go beyond your newfound observance – I still think Judaism is the issue. But even as I struggle against so much of what you're doing, I do stand back from time to time and find myself respecting it. I guess I feel conflicted. I need a little space to sort things out for myself.

But I'm willing to try at this point because I believe we belong together. Even though your outward observance has changed, I still see the same person I married underneath – the one I thought had a connection with God from the moment I met him.

I'd like to expand on what you said about Paul. The connection I saw in you was not childish. It was child-like, meaning it was pure, unpretentious and real. The Judaism of kosher-style food is childish because it's masquerading as something it's not. I understand why you want authenticity. I just wish there were an easier way to get it.

When my sister Angela was around Micah's age, my mother walked outside one day to find her sitting on the tractor and looking up at the sky, laughing like there was no tomorrow. When Mom asked her what was so funny, Angela said, "Oh, I was just laughing at God."

In so many ways, I wish I could go back to that simple, child-like faith. When I was a child, I just talked to God. I didn't need to worry that my faith would collide with my family.

Yes, I want to try. But not simply to avoid devastating pain for the three of us. I want to try because every part of me says we belong together. Remember the old saying, "Love conquers all." So far, it's conquered everything that's come along in our marriage. There has to be a way to conquer this mess as well.

Love,

Gayle

᳇ఞ

June 19, 2001

Dear Gayle,

I called Shana, the therapist, and we have an appointment. She seemed nice, and wasn't fazed a bit when I described our situation.

After I hung up, I thought of something I recently heard from one of the rabbinical candidates at Temple Shalom. Cherie has worked a lot with intermarried families, and we were discussing the best ways to reach out to them.

I've never heard another rabbi admit this: "You know, no matter how good you are at outreach, there are some intermarried families who don't want to be reached out to." The reason, she said, is that an interfaith couple carries certain underlying, and often unspoken, assumptions about religion. According to Cherie, by reaching out to them, the Jewish community threatens those assumptions, some of which undergird the marriage itself.

This got me thinking – what are our underlying assumptions? Clearly, my spiritual path has been threatening some of those assumptions. At the same time, we're on the same page with some of our assumptions in ways some other interfaith couples are not.

This may be a good place to begin with Shana. Articulate our assumptions, define them, determine which are essential, which can be changed and which can't, and see if we can bring any new assumptions to the table that will speak better to where we are now.

Love,

Harold

ે✷✷

Part IV
The Road Ahead . . .

Not I, nor anyone else can travel that road for you.
You must travel it by yourself.
It is not far. It is within reach.
Perhaps you have been on it since you were born,
and did not know.

Walt Whitman

September 6, 2001

Dear Harold,

You're right – the path you've taken has been threatening the religious and many of the life-style assumptions with which we entered our marriage. Eleven years ago, I never dreamed you'd be asking me to "hold the milk" in the potatoes when I serve chicken. I never dreamed you'd refuse to take my best friend's photo on a Saturday. I never dreamed I'd be raising a Jewish child and feel increasingly left out of my Jewish husband's Judaism.

The other day, I opened up to Melissa about some of the goings-on in our home. She handed me one of those relationship books that describe "what really works" with men. This doesn't look promising, I thought. But one chapter leapt off the page: "Will You Do What it Takes?" The chapter claims that if the goal is to succeed in your "long-term, committed relationship," then you have to put into perspective those things that are interfering with your success. "Think about what you really want, what is truly important and valuable to you."

What I want most is that the three of us are together as a family – and much more than that – that the three of us are in sync and growing in our relationship rather than discovering one day that mashed potatoes have revealed groundshaking, existential issues.

Does that necessarily mean I would need to become Jewish? It can't mean that. I can't just become Jewish, unless it's what I really want. If it's forced, we'll have much bigger problems than mashed potatoes.

I started thinking – to be a Jew, a religious Jew anyway, would mean that I couldn't work on Shabbat. That's not so easy for someone who performs, often on Friday nights.

I started thinking about how music has been such a big part of my life. I have to keep singing. I know God gave me this voice to use, not to give up the chance to sing.

Working in a church isn't the greatest thing for a religious Jew to be doing. But I wasn't looking for this job in the first place. I still love directing the choir and playing the organ. What would I replace it with? Teaching in a Christian school doesn't present the same issues since it doesn't involve Christian worship. Shana said there are Christians who teach at Yeshiva University, so why not the reverse?

Wait! Why am I thinking about this? I'm not planning to convert, just to find a way for our religions to happily co-exist in the same house.

Then it hit me. I've been making my own changes, unconsciously, but far more than I had realized. More often than not, I'm with you and Micah at synagogue. At first, I went because it seemed like the right thing to do if we were going to raise a Jewish child. But now, I find myself looking forward to going.

Even though the milk/meat thing was a shock initially, I've been buying kosher food for a long time. At this point, I reflexively look for that little U inside the O that tells me an Orthodox Union kashrut inspector has given his sign-off.

Looking for kosher symbols in the supermarket aisle and trekking to synagogue is one thing. But what do I believe?

This is what hit me the hardest. I now realize that, for many years, the most important part of being a church musician has been the music itself. I can't remember the last time I entered a church when I wasn't performing or watching someone else perform.

I do enjoy making the music meaningful to the congregation. But I wonder if they've caught on that they've been listening only to choir anthems that use texts from the Hebrew Bible. It's not something I planned. It just happened over time, without my even being aware of it. But somewhere along the line, leaving out the texts about Jesus felt more comfortable – and so I did.

A few months ago, I started refusing communion.

I didn't do any of these things for you or Micah. I did them because they felt right – for me.

As I look back on the past couple of years, I see how much Jewish observance I've already taken on. I don't know if I can take on everything, or if I want to. What's clear is that I have a lot of thinking to do, and I need to relate to this independent of, and not in reaction to, your own process.

What's also clear is that, wherever this strange path leads us, we belong together as a family.

Love,

Gayle

ം⊰ക

September 8, 2001

Dear Gayle,

I'm not sure which is more surprising – that you've deleted all reference to Jesus from the music, or that no one at United Church has noticed that you've deleted all reference to Jesus (I know that if a Cantor *added* a reference to Jesus, a Jewish congregation would notice right away).

Seriously, I had no idea so much was happening underneath the surface. I guess this is new territory for both of us.

We may still be in different places, but we share a number of underlying assumptions. First, I can't ask you to convert. If you ever did convert, it would need to come from you.

Second, becoming Jewish is a big commitment. It can be a wonderful journey, but it's a long one, and to take it lightly would be at your peril.

Third, when you or I talk about becoming Jewish or living a Jewish life, we agree that that means a religious life, a life infused with Torah. For me, as I've said, there's not much point to do otherwise. For a person who converts, even more so. What meaning would a Jewish identity with minimal religion hold for someone not born Jewish? A born Jew might substitute Torah with bagels, politics, pride in the "tribe," or a sentimental nostalgia masquerading as "tradition." Why anyone not born Jewish would give up their religion for any of these, however, is beyond me.

On Sunday, the Search Committee interviewed a Reconstructionist rabbi, expanding our ever-widening spectrum of candidates in search of we don't know what.

He was honest about his own spiritual leanings when the Committee asked him how he, as a liberal Reconstructionist rabbi, would fit into a Conservative congregation. He replied that, although he would honor the rules of the Conservative movement, he is still a Reconstructionist rabbi. For example, he said, "My family observes Shabbat in a way that works for us. We've been known to drive to a movie on Shabbat afternoon. I think you should know that."

Without a hint of irony, Michael piped up, "As Conservative Jews, we go to the mall on Shabbat. But we don't want to see our rabbi there."

We expect our rabbi to be observant so that we don't have to – excuse me?

Observing the mitzvot is not simply following a set of rules. It's a way of life – one that is as relevant today as when the Israelites stood at Mount Sinai 3,500 years ago. No amount of volunteering at weekly Bingo, getting the synagogue newsletter out, or spending too much on a Bar Mitzvah party will ever compensate for that.

And that brings me back to the first and second assumptions. To convert in a way that's meaningful is serious business, and is something I can't ask of you. If you ever chose to convert, I suspect neither of us would be at the mall on Saturday. And with all we've been through, if you ever chose to convert, I would need to know as much as you that I was not the reason.

Love,

Harold

ॐ∽

October 29, 2001

Dear Harold,

For years, I've been saying it would be nice to learn Hebrew. It feels strange all of a sudden to be doing it. We're starting at the very beginning, saying the sound of each letter over and over until we're comfortable enough to move on to the next letter.

Ann Geller has to be the most patient Hebrew teacher in the world. Several people in the class are retirees who finally have the time to learn Hebrew. There's a man with a thick Brooklyn accent who learned to pronounce Hebrew with an "s" where Israelis put a "t". Then there are a few Russian immigrants, who still sound like they're speaking Russian when they say the Hebrew. The odd mix makes for some interesting moments.

It struck me at the first class that Hebrew is like a parallel universe – everyone knew without being told to start at the back of the book and turn the pages backward. Except that here, backward is forward.

I hadn't imagined I'd be taking a beginner's Hebrew class in an Orthodox synagogue, but so much has happened lately that I would never have imagined. After going to Young Israel of Brookline for months (in between going to Temple Shalom), you suddenly decided to see what another Orthodox synagogue is like and ended up at Kadima Toras Moshe. That the synagogue President remembered your name, and after Shabbat found your number in the phone book and called you, is amazing.

Even more amazing is that he called you to tell you about the classes at the synagogue. When he mentioned the beginner's Hebrew class, I don't know why you, almost without thinking, said you knew basic Hebrew, "but I think my wife might be interested."

Since I've started to get to know the people in the class, I thought I ought to make the trek with you on Shabbat morning. So far, so good, but I wonder if I can continue to pull this off. How long can I stay incognito, without them knowing that I'm not an Orthodox Jew – or not a Jew, period, for that matter?

I don't want to "come out" because I don't want people to start wondering why I'm there, or what my motives are. I just want to see what it is that's been taking up such a big part of your life. I want to see why Orthodox Judaism is pulling on you so strongly.

The past few weeks of Hebrew classes already have made a difference – every so often, I can even figure out where I'm supposed to be in the prayer book. Sitting next to Ann and watching where she is does give me a leg up. But I can't see how I'll ever read Hebrew well enough to keep up with the lightning pace of the service. So for now, I just read the English whenever I need to and try to stay on the right page.

Whenever I start feeling uncomfortable, someone inevitably appears and puts me at ease. Women I've never met come up to me to say hi. I haven't been around many Orthodox women before, but they seem so grounded. People at the Kiddush show genuine interest in us. And already several families have invited us to join them for Shabbat lunch.

Best of all, Micah loves going to the children's service. Never mind participating in the service – he's thrilled that there are scores of children everywhere you turn. I can't imagine how we'll get him back to Temple Shalom.

For now, anyway, this Orthodox synagogue seems like a good place for the three of us to be together on Saturday mornings. Although you're still going to Young Israel sometimes, and putting in appearances at Temple Shalom since you're on the Search Committee – you may want to consider narrowing things down a bit.

Love,

Gayle

☙❧

November 1, 2001

Dear Gayle,

Groucho Marks said, "I wouldn't want to join any club that would have me as a member." That about sums it up.

Aish, Young Israel, Kadima Toras Moshe – all these places are so full of life in a way that I've had a hard time finding in other parts of the Jewish world. The people at Aish introduced me to the idea that being observant can be joyful. And although they never exactly expressed their approval of interfaith marriage, they genuinely wanted both of us there. All the singing, the warmth, the heartfelt prayer I found at Young Israel gave me a new level of enthusiasm for going to synagogue. The people at Kadima Toras Moshe, although they don't know our situation, have embraced us.

So with all of this positive reinforcement, and your new-found interest in exploring – wherever this path may lead – I got lulled into thinking that I, even we, had a place in the Orthodox world. I've spent more time at Young Israel than anywhere else, so it seemed natural to call Rabbi Gewirtz and explore the possibilities a little. It all seemed so promising on the phone. Yes, of course he would be happy to meet with me to discuss whatever was on my mind. No, it didn't matter that I'm not a member of the synagogue. When would I like to come over?

I grew less confident as I walked through his office doorway. Books, books, books everywhere. More than I had seen in any other rabbi's office I had visited. And virtually all of them were in Hebrew.

Rabbi Gewirtz' easy manner put me at ease, and I quickly got over his intimidating bookshelves and found myself opening up. I told him about my journey, Micah's enthusiasm, and your nascent interest in Judaism although stopping short of conversion. He listened attentively, and seemed to care about what I was telling him the way an old friend would. He applauded my newfound commitment to Judaism, and encouraged me to continue learning and growing. All that worry for nothing.

And then came the bucket of ice cold water. With a tone that was at once compassionate and matter-of-fact, I heard him say, "You need to understand this community that you are trying to be part of. Shabbat is a way of life here. 95% of the children in this synagogue go to day school. There are no intermarried families.

"As long as you are intermarried, you won't be able to fit in here. If Gayle were interested in converting, then you would have a chance. But as things are now, it won't work."

I asked if he was telling me not to come to Young Israel anymore. He said that this absolutely was not the case. "But," he said, "you have to consider whether you will just be creating a more difficult situation for yourself. You really have to give some thought to where all of this is going to lead."

Rabbi Gewirtz may have been uncomfortably direct. But he's right. Now that I've experienced these communities, I can't imagine continuing at Temple Shalom past my commitment to the Search Committee. I cannot make my home in a Jewish community where either my observance will brand me as a freak, or I will have to suppress the Jewish life I feel I should be living in order to fit in. And I can't imagine raising Micah that way. As he grows up, we won't be able to hide the hypocrisy he will see through in an instant and from which he will run far and fast.

But this isn't only about me and my needs, or even Micah's. It's also about you. Once the novelty wore off of finding a synagogue with a good Cantor and nice people, you became just as tired of the lack of observance and unwillingness to grow that pervades Temple Shalom. You've found Kadima-Toras Moshe to be a much closer fit in every way – the feeling of community, the level of commitment, the values, and what it can offer Micah.

But we've been there, as you said, "incognito." If we lived on our own island, this would be easy. But we have to find a way to live in a community – one that we want to be part of and that will also have us as members. Where does this path lead for a church organist who seems to be leaving the Christian fold, a wannabe Orthodox Jew, and a little boy who is too young to understand his parents' dilemma?

That almost sounds like the beginning of one of those "there was a rabbi and a priest" jokes. Unfortunately, it's no joke. It's our lives. I know there's a solution somewhere in all this. But I have no idea what it is.

Love,

Harold

ॐঞ্চ

November 1, 2001

Dear Harold,

We're trying to raise a Jewish child as best we can. I'm studying Hebrew and trying to learn the ins and outs of an Orthodox synagogue. We're even sending Micah to Shaloh House Pre-School – if a Chabad school can create a space for us, why not the rest of the Orthodox community? I can't believe God wants to take a family that is trying so hard and throw them into an unresolvable crisis.

I see intermarried couples who are raising their children in minimally Jewish settings, and no one complains. Why does trying to raise our child with a serious version of Judaism mean that we have a big problem? If we opted to raise Micah with a token amount of Judaism, where his chances of taking it seriously would be close to zero, then the Jewish community (outside of Orthodoxy, anyway), would welcome us with open arms, and tell us how grateful they are that we are raising a Jewish child. But the minute we try to go beyond that, the more committed Jews tell us it's not enough.

Where is this all going to lead? I have no idea, and at this stage, it doesn't matter. I told you that I've realized I'm not a believing Christian anymore, that now I need to think and explore. But I've spent my whole life relating to God as a Christian. This is not like switching from Crest to Colgate – it takes time if it's going to mean anything. That is, if any switching is going to take place. Church services have been a big part of my musical life, and I don't yet see a fulfilling way to replace that. Not being a Christian doesn't mean I have to be Jewish.

Whatever I decide, I've got to do it for myself, not because you or the rabbi or anyone else is worrying about where it's going to lead. Perhaps some Orthodox Jews would be happier if we faded from view, went to a Reform temple, or became a statistic marked "unaffiliated." I'm not going anywhere. That I'm frequenting an Orthodox synagogue, happy that my child is there, and studying Hebrew should be a clue that I'm interested in exploring this – but on my terms, at my pace, and in a way that doesn't require me to give up everything I've ever known. Please stop worrying where all this is going to lead and give me some space.

Love,

Gayle

৵৽

November 2, 2001

Dear Gayle,

I don't want you to give up everything you've ever known. And I don't believe you will, no matter what you do. Beneath the Torah-learning, Shabbat-observing, kosher food-eating person I seem to be becoming, I am still me. In fact, this little journey has drawn me closer to the real me. Wherever you go with this, or not, you won't become anyone except who you truly are.

I guess I'm nervous. Yes, you've started making unconscious changes in your own life. But you also, until recently, felt a lot of resistance to the changes in my life. How can I know that your path isn't influenced by mine, that the decisions you come to are yours and not borne of a desire to make problems go away? I'm seeking assurance that I know you can't give me yet.

I'm scared – what if the problems don't go away? Yes, much of the Jewish world outside Orthodoxy celebrates interfaith families who raise their children even with a minimalist Judaism. But my visits to Aish tell a different story – lots of young people from interfaith homes trying to find themselves, trying to understand who they are and where they fit in, trying not to feel like they are letting down one of their parents if they choose the other one's religion.

We've both seen the vast gulf at Temple Shalom between converts who did it for their spouse, and those who converted because they want to be Jewish. I would never be happy if I somehow pushed you into converting, if you went along this path thinking it was your own but it was really mine. It would never feel real to either of us. Nor to Micah.

I know I need to just back off and let the path unfold. Every session with Shana, I say that our issues are about religion. I keep imagining that, as an Orthodox therapist, she will have no choice but to agree with me. Instead, Shana ducks the religion ball I keep throwing out, and insists that our issues are about communication. I just sit there, incredulous that this Orthodox Jew who is supposed to be helping us doesn't focus more on the fact that we are intermarried, that we have different backgrounds, that we're in different places.

Instead, Shana's mantra is communication. As if . . . as if this spot we find ourselves in would go away if we just talked more directly and listened more empathetically. As if better communication would move us beyond theological concepts, beyond our inability to find a religious community anywhere that will work for both of us, beyond how we explain our family to a little boy in a way that sounds the least bit coherent

Perhaps Shana is not saying that communication is a cure-all, but a starting point. So I'll keep working on communicating, let the path unfold, and try not to look down when the path begins to feel like a tightrope.

Love,

Harold

ॐ◌

November 28, 2001

Dear Harold,

Do you think anyone figured out who we "really" are? Did I "pass" as an Orthodox Jewish woman? This was a Shabbat I'm sure not to forget.

Online, the place sounded ideal – a kosher hotel nestled in the Catskills. A weekend to ourselves, with your parents watching Micah, leaving us free to delve into the world of Orthodox Judaism.

Entering the Homawack Hotel is like entering another era – unfortunately not an era to which anyone wishes to return. The shag carpet that blanketed the lobby must have been put down when disco and leisure suits reigned, and judging by the stale air, I don't think it's been cleaned since then.

Then there were the rows of tables set atop the shag carpet, with vendors hawking Judaica and souvenirs. I don't imagine they allow that at the Ritz. I suppose Micah will enjoy the 9/11 NYC Fireman's hat they convinced us to buy, and we'll enjoy the Shabbat tablecloth.

Once I got beyond the hotel itself – and admittedly, that wasn't easy – I had a great time, maybe the first time we've observed an entire Shabbat together. There's something beautiful about taking 25 hours to disconnect from the workaday world.

And we sure learned a lot. We learned how to negotiate a Shabbat dinner properly by watching our tablemates (and sometimes by being

*gently corrected by our tablemates). We already knew to wash our hands
before the blessing on the challah, but we both forgot that we aren't supposed to talk between the washing and the blessing, since they are considered as one unit (that was where we again relied on our tablemates to
gently correct us). You learned how to conduct the blessings for the wine
and challah (again, with a bit of gentle correcting). And I learned that
a freshly purchased hat from the sale rack at Target works just fine for a
weekend at the Homawack (I'm sure all the other women paid far more
for their hats and wigs).*

*The Shabbat morning service is still a challenge, and the Homa-
wack mechitza didn't help. At least at Kadimah Toras Moshe, while the
men and women may be separated by a mechitza, that mechitza is built
in such a way so that the women can partially see what's going on. At the
Homawack, I couldn't see a thing. I can understand the value of being
separate – I can see your point that that separateness creates a very different energy. But they can create a separation without making me feel like
I'm in a different room.*

*I saw one woman with five daughters in tow. Just before the start
of the prayer where people step back and then up again, they did it together,
totally in sync. There's something hauntingly beautiful about five women
from the same family stepping back and then walking forward together to
approach God in prayer. As I was lost in this thought, a woman who had
come late asked me where we were in the service. I didn't have the heart to
tell her that I was the one person in the room with no clue.*

*Saturday night showed me what might be possible, and what still
seems hopelessly out of reach. I must admit that until "Simply Tzfat" from
Israel took the stage, I had never thought to put "Breslov Hassidim" and
"amazing musicians" together in the same sentence.*

*The violinist's story enthralled me – how he had made it as a musi-
cian in New York City, but found all his work drying up once he became
religious and couldn't accept any gigs on Shabbat. How everything went
downhill, to the point where he even lost his violin. How a new violin appeared almost out of nowhere, marking the beginning of his ascent to a new
musical career that allows him to be an Orthodox Jew.*

*I began to see myself finding my own musical niche as an Ortho-
dox Jewish woman. I thought about how surprisingly comfortable I felt
this weekend playing that role, and wondering what it would be like if it*

turned into the real thing. I remembered Shana saying that when you make a decision, sometimes the things you need to support your decision fall into place.

Then reality came knocking on the door. I'm not playing in a klezmer band – I'm singing opera. The last time I checked, there are no opera companies that cease performing on Shabbat to accommodate any Orthodox Jewish singers who happen to be around. And as strange as I still find it, there are some Orthodox men who, for reasons of modesty, will not watch a woman perform. If I were to convert, no Orthodox hotel would be inviting me to tell my life story in between singing the songs I love.

I thought back to Shabbat lunch, when a woman at our table asked how long we've been observant (I said we were still in process and you were a little ahead of me!), and why I teach girls how to sing. She couldn't understand why girls (Orthodox girls, anyway) would learn to sing if they weren't talented enough to do it professionally.

Ok, so I won't be crushed if I don't get a gig at the Homawack, and I've taught so many students who love singing even though they'll never make a career of it.

But what about my career? If I were a computer analyst, or a lawyer, or an English teacher, or a million other things, I could just focus on the warmth I felt this weekend. All it would take would be to negotiate with my employer to leave a little early on Friday afternoons, and I could just enjoy the beauty of performing the mitzvot, and of relating directly to God.

But I'm not a million other things. All I've ever wanted to do is to sing. Shana may be right – the right things may fall into place. This weekend, I felt myself wanting those things to fall into place – I just can't see yet how they will.

In the meantime, I've got performances coming up, and I need to get over my cold – which I know is from that stale shag carpet.

Love,

Gayle

๛

Parshat Mikeitz – Dec. 15, 2001

Dear Gayle,

Since speaking with Rabbi Gewirtz, I haven't been back to Young Israel. But this Shabbat morning, for some reason I woke up wanting to go. Sitting among the 400 other people in the congregation, I felt like the rabbi had prepared his words just for me.

In this week's Torah portion, Joseph is removed from jail after the butler suddenly remembers him and tells Pharoah that Joseph may be able to interpret his dreams. As Rabbi Gewirtz explained, when Joseph is taken from jail, his prisoner clothes are exchanged for a new uniform, representing his dramatic change of status. The Torah describes Joseph being taken from his prison cell, where just a few moments before he seemed destined to reside permanently, by saying he was "rushed" to Pharoah. His whole world transformed, as Rabbi Turtletaub would say, "in the blink of an eye."

Often, Rabbi Gewirtz explained, things are happening behind the scenes or underneath the surface that aren't apparent to us. And then – all of a sudden – things are "rushed," things turn around completely. Joseph's story shows us that no matter what things looked like yesterday or how stuck we are in yesterday, today could be so different.

I know I've doubted you. I've doubted your decision to explore Judaism, and now your thoughts about converting. I'm sorry. I only wanted to be sure that this was real, that you were doing this for you, and not for me. I want you to be happy. I don't want you to become Jewish for any reason other than it's what you want. And I don't want you to sacrifice your music to do it.

Coming home from Young Israel, I thought about what you've said during our meetings with Shana these past few months. I thought about how things changed so much once we started talking, really talking. When we started opening up to each other, I think we started to be open with ourselves about what we want deep down. Once you no longer felt the need to resist my increased observance done without your consent, it freed you up to look at Judaism anew.

I thought beyond the past few months, to our first years together. You fasted our first Yom Kippur together. You observed Passover from the time we met, dutifully carrying your box of matzah with you to work at Colonial Hills Church. It was you who suggested we start lighting candles on Friday night. It was you who didn't want a Christmas tree anyway, regardless of my feelings about it. It was you who said you couldn't convert because of the music, which puzzled me at the time, but which I now realize means that you must have been thinking about it on some level.

There were plenty of earlier signs that both of us missed. But I guess things happen when they're meant to, in their own time. Like Rabbi Gewirtz' description of Joseph, things were happening underneath the surface with both of us that are only now ready to come out.

I acknowledge that it is not for me to say what your process has been, what has been going on underneath the surface, or what you truly feel. But you have been telling me lately what you feel and what you want to do. I know now that I need to listen, and I need to trust you.

Love,

Harold

&⊱⊰&

January 27, 2002

Dear Harold,

Lately, I've been searching for myself in books. It's one thing to say I want to convert. It's quite another to put myself in front of a rabbi, and have to explain why I want to turn my life on its head. Scary. Overwhelming. Even exotic – I've wondered how common this is. I'd love to speak with people who've been down this road. I've met converts – but no Orthodox ones.

For now, books are safe. I can pick them up and put them down at will, and I don't have to fear that they'll reject me or say something I can't handle. Well, even if a book does say something I can't handle, I can close it without feeling embarrassed that the book will see me getting emotional.

In books, I've already found half a dozen of the Orthodox converts I've been looking for in real life. There's "Ordained to Be a Jew" by John Scalimonti, and "So Strange My Path" by Abraham Carmel, both ex-Catholic priests who found their home in Orthodox Judaism. I've since learned there are more than a few former Christian clergy whose difficult questioning led them out of Christianity and into Judaism. Then there's "The Lord Will Gather Me In" by David Klinghoffer, who was born to a Christian woman, adopted as a baby by a Reform Jewish family, and made his way to Orthodox Judaism in his uncompromising search for authenticity (undergoing no fewer than three circumcisions along the way!).

If someone from Eastern Nazarene College or United Church were to come to our home today and peruse our bookshelf, I can only imagine what they would think. Of all the conversion accounts I've read, the two in which I most see myself are "My Sister, the Jew" by Ahuvah Gray and "To Play With Fire" by Tova Mordechai. Like me, both Gray and Mordechai began in leadership positions in Evangelical churches.

Ahuvah Gray is the granddaughter of Mississippi sharecroppers. She grew up surrounded by devout Christians, ultimately became a minister and started taking groups to Israel. Falling in love with the country, she began to study Hebrew. That's when everything started to unravel. As she read Biblical passages in the original, she found discrepancies with the Christian translations and with the Church doctrine she had absorbed from the time she learned to talk. When no one could satisfactorily answer her questions, Gray began a search that took her to the heart of an Orthodox community in Jerusalem, where she lives today.

Tova Mordechai led and taught in an Evangelical church in England. Technically not a convert, her story reads like one. Her father was the church movement's leader, while her mother had been born Jewish but converted to Christianity when she met her father. From an early age, Tova found herself fascinated by Jews, something her father actively discouraged.

Eventually, she too broke with the church and went on to become an Ortho-dox Jew – not without a few bumps along the way.

Reading their accounts, I want to meet them – or at least to meet someone who has stood in my shoes and is now standing in Orthodox Jew-ish shoes.

Love,

Gayle

ॐ

February 6, 2002

Dear Gayle,

The problem with all of your convert books is that I want to read them too. Each account is a revelation about my own path as a born Jew.

I think these accounts – at times incredible and always fascinating – should be required reading for every born Jew. A born Jew doesn't have to jump through any hoops. A born Jew can know nothing about the Bible, not be able to tell an aleph from a bet, never grace the doorway of a synagogue, and never observe a Shabbat his entire life. A born Jew can eat ham drowned in butter topped with shrimp, hold Buddhists in great esteem while holding Jews who talk to God in contempt, and see more truth in the New York Times than the Talmud. A born Jew can base his whole identity on fighting against everyone "out there" who dislikes Jews, never giving a thought to what makes him a Jew from within.

All that – and he's still a Jew. Because, after all, he was born a Jew.

And he will angrily denounce the intolerant soul who dares to suggest he lacks a thing as a Jew. He has his shrimp, his Buddhist meditation, his anti-Semitism, and his New York Times – who would have the audacity to say that what he does is any less Jewish than someone whose whole life is guided by the Torah?

Because, after all, he was born a Jew. He doesn't have to *do* anything.

Along comes the convert to shatter this born Jew's comfort zone. The convert studies Judaism, sometimes for years. She has to knock on doors, sometimes even knock them down – and be approved for admission. She can't share this born Jew's ambivalence about Jewish identity. She can't do whatever she wants and call it "being a Jew." She has to hear the call of Sinai, break through every barrier to get there, and live the intensive Jewish life this born Jew shuns. She can't take a thing for granted.

I'm beginning to understand why some of the Jews I've met, especially some who aren't religious, have trouble accepting converts or understanding their motivations. Meeting the convert is like looking in the mirror of what could be. A mirror that doesn't permit the excuses they can throw up to a more observant born Jew.

The mirror of the convert mocks the born Jew who says it's too hard, it's not necessary, it's just a cultural thing, it's really all the same as long as you try to be a good person. A few weeks ago, I heard someone extolling the virtues of Jewish culture, in the middle of which came the throwaway line, "I wish I could be observant." You wish? What's stopping you? The mirror reflects back someone who's thought this through, who's worked at this for years, who is in love with a tradition she was not automatically born into, who's stopped at nothing to reach her destination – the mirror tells the born Jew that he could overcome his own obstacles if only he wanted it enough.

So what else are you reading these days?

Love,

Harold

❧⸙

February 14, 2002

Dear Harold,

What am I reading? I've read more in the last two months than in the past two years. Inside, this feels absolutely right. My heart is in this. But I want my mind to be too.

The converts' accounts all speak of falling in love with Judaism, of Christianity no longer making sense to them, and of the long path they walked to join the Jewish people. While they do speak here and there of their intellectual issues with Christianity, unbridgeable theological gaps, and translations that don't add up, they don't dwell on it.

Maybe they want to talk more about why they embraced Judaism than what they found missing in Christianity – that's probably as it should be. I find myself doing the same thing. But I want something more than "just because it feels right" to be the reason I stopped taking communion, eliminated every reference to Jesus in the church choir, started learning Hebrew, started attending an Orthodox synagogue, and am now turning my life upside down.

In a bookstore on Harvard Street in Brookline, nestled among the Judaica stores and kosher restaurants, I stumbled upon some answers from an ex-Catholic priest. Geza Vermes was born in the 1920s to a European Jewish family that became Catholic. Vermes went all the way, taking his vows for the priesthood. He is recognized as one of the leading authorities on the Dead Sea Scrolls, but as a result of all his research, ultimately left the church and reclaimed his Jewish identity. He has also since become one of the world's leading scholars on Jesus within the historical context of first century Judaism. In short, he's a good guide to take on the road beyond "just because it feels right."

Without going into all of the details, most of what he says makes perfect sense. The differing accounts and approaches throughout the New Testament simply cannot be reconciled, and the figure of Jesus rings most true as a very human religious leader in ancient Israel – not as a messiah figure that is so conceptually different from what "messiah" meant at that time – and certainly not as the son of God or God himself. The rationalizations I've read to the contrary are – well – rationalizations.

But agreeing with Vermes takes me only so far. It can explain why I'm refusing communion, but not specifically why I am praying at an Orthodox synagogue. That's where the emotional part comes back into the picture. Judaism does make sense to me intellectually – but beyond providing satisfying answers to my questions, it "just feels right."

From another New Testament scholar, I've discovered that maybe it's not so important – or easy – to isolate the intellectual from the emotional. Maybe after all the probing, questioning, analyzing and thinking, there's a part that can never be explained, that "just feels right."

Everything at Paula Fredriksen's talk last week at Hebrew College reinforced what I've been reading in the Vermes book. Fredriksen, like Vermes, is one of the world's leading scholars on Jesus. Unlike Vermes, Fredriksen was born into a Christian family, and today is an Orthodox Jew. But it was what she said in the Q&A that stuck with me.

"It all started during a volleyball game at Princeton." I must admit that, among the many accounts of converts I've now read, not one has identified a volleyball game as the origin of her quest to become an Orthodox Jew.

Fredriksen described how, as a graduate student at Princeton, she was playing volleyball with a bunch of biology and physics students, discussing to what extent science can explain things in between lobs over the net. After much back and forth – both the ball and the discussion – they concluded that science can very closely describe natural phenomena, but cannot ultimately explain anything.

Absolutely true. Science might try to "explain" the origins of the universe. But science is only describing in minute detail what happened (or at least what scientists today think happened – the next generation may offer an entirely different description). It isn't "explaining" a thing about why it happened, why we're here, or what's the purpose of it all.

The audience hung on Fredriksen's every word, awaiting the next part of her story. And then she hurriedly said, "And from there, it was just a natural progression to becoming an Orthodox Jew."

It's quite a leap even to go from the realization that science doesn't explain our existence to the conclusion that our existence has a purpose. It's a much greater leap to conclude that there is a God, that He created the world and everything in it, that He singled out a certain people and gave them the Torah, and that the Torah's commandments are binding on every Jew.

I can give my own reasons why I believe all of those things to be true. Fredriksen is brilliant. I suspect she could speak for hours about her own very well-thought-out answers rather than reducing her Jewish journey to one sentence. Maybe she didn't want to dwell on her journey, or considers it to be too personal. But I suspect that at the end of the day, like me, she chose to become Jewish "just because it feels right."

And with that, I'm going to start looking for a rabbi who can help me make this long journey official.

Love,

Gayle

ৎ৵৵

February 18, 2002

Dear Gayle,

In my own journey, I've gone through this exact back-and-forth process. One week, I'm comparing Jewish beliefs with academic Biblical criticism theories, looking for the holes in each and coming to my own conclusions. The next week, I'm losing myself in the warm fuzzy feeling of some newly discovered Jewish practice. At the end of the day, there's something incredibly deep here, something that academic theories can't begin to address. Still, our minds need more than warm, fuzzy feelings – otherwise, who's to say that those people who believe the earth was started by purple space aliens don't have just as good a claim? But our intellect takes us just so far, and the rest of the journey can only be fueled by faith.

I recently heard two rabbis debate this very issue. One proposed that our spiritual lives are all about what we can sense objectively, while the other argued strenuously that we can have confidence in our faith precisely because of what we can't see. Only, they didn't put it quite that way. And truth be told, they didn't know they were debating each other.

A few months ago, I went to a talk by Rabbi Wein, the rabbi from that Jewish Renewal synagogue we visited a couple of years ago. He's a great speaker, and his topic was how to make Judaism meaningful, so I figured I had nothing to lose.

"Where is God?," he asked. "God is in my finger. God is in my right arm." He went on to say that, although such words might sound heretical, God really exists inside each of us and in the actions we do.

True enough, up to a point. Judaism certainly puts a premium on action, and on God's presence manifesting itself in our actions. But something's missing here, I thought. That's not the whole story. God doesn't just exist in my little finger.

Then I went to Rabbi Glaser's Torah study at Aish last week. "How do I know God exists?" Rabbi Glaser began. "Because I have fingertips."

Yes, God exists in each of us. That's part of what makes us human. But we participate in the world – we didn't create it and we don't run it. As Rabbi Glaser went on to explain, God gave us fingers to do our part. But we have fingertips – we are limited. God is not.

As I bounced back and forth between fingers and fingertips, I suddenly wondered why any of this matters. Life was easier before. We weren't reading all these books. We weren't working through all these issues. We weren't thinking about studying with rabbis and changing our food and our dishes, and blocking out one day a week. What happened?

Micah's entry into our family would be the obvious answer. It would be impossible for anyone with even a drop of religious feeling to remain unmoved watching him bound through the synagogue on Shabbat morning like it's his home, or hearing him explain with breathless excitement what he learned at Shaloh House Pre-School.

But the obvious answer is not always correct. Micah's embrace of all things Jewish has been a catalyst. But a catalyst can only magnify what already exists. Intellectually, certain things over time started to make sense and others didn't. Emotionally, as you put it so well, this just feels right. What is it that Micah has helped to unearth?

I can never know with certainty what experience lit the spark that brought me to this place. Or perhaps, as the Jewish Sages claim, my soul stood at Sinai, but it has been waiting all this time for the rest of me to wake up.

Whatever the cause, as I've thought about the fingers/ fingertips debate, one moment plays itself over and over in my mind. I barely noticed it at the time, but underneath my awareness, it drove home why the intellectual and the emotional, the fingers and the fingertips, ultimately do not conflict.

It was a Sunday morning in May back at the old Monroe Temple of Liberal Judaism. Instead of playing ball with my friends, I was stuck in the temple's basement, along with half a dozen other fifteen-year olds. And one rabbi.

This final year of Confirmation classes was supposed to be the real thing. No more slideshows or discussions of UFOs. We knew this was serious because Rabbi Metzger was our teacher. And you didn't get any more serious than Rabbi Metzger.

Rabbi Kurt Metzger's short stature belied his imposing persona. He had led the Reform community of Nuremberg, Germany as its last rabbi before the Nazi inferno. The same Nuremberg where the Nazis' crimes against humanity were later put on display for the world to see.

Rabbi Metzger grew up in a Germany that offered Jews the world, only to see that world reduced to a concentration camp. Before the Nazis were through, Rabbi Metzger had spent time behind the barbed wire of Buchenwald.

Although he spoke often about the Holocaust, it was not his subject on that May morning. The issue he put before the class was whether God exists.

The sophomoric discussion weaved its way to one rigid conclusion – God could not possibly exist. If there is a God, some of the students reasoned, then there couldn't be so much evil in the world. Science has explained everything, so we don't need God. God is not real, but a conceptual crutch people use when they can't explain how or why something happens.

So the arguments went. The freethinking tenth graders could grasp only what they could see. And their eyes could not admit the possibility of God. So caught up were they in their newfound atheism that the rabbi, despite his strong personality, struggled to gain his footing.

One student contemptuously demanded of Rabbi Metzger, "Rabbi, do *you* believe in God?" The time for reasoned intellectual discussion had passed. We waited impatiently for the rabbi's answer. And then the tables turned.

The last Rabbi of Nuremberg, survivor of Buchenwald, stood before us.

"Yes, I believe in God."

His eyes had witnessed the unthinkable. A world that stood by silently. Man treating his fellow man as animal, and becoming animal as a result. But in a voice that filled the room with its quiet conviction:

"Yes, I believe in God. I *know* there is a God."

God would have had no place in that room if one considered what Rabbi Metzger's eyes had witnessed. Yet, that May morning, his presence somehow bore eloquent testimony to the opposite conclusion.

What his eyes witnessed didn't define him. It reminded him of what he was not, of his essential humanity. It reminded him that beyond the fingertips of the Nazis, God exists – and that we need him, both within us and beyond us.

Abraham Joshua Heschel, who lost his mother and sisters to the Holocaust, also weighed in on the fingers/fingertips debate: "I say that this world in itself is so fascinatingly mysterious, so challengingly marvelous, that not to realize that there is more than I see, that there is endlessly more than I can express or even conceive, is just being underdeveloped intellectually."

It would be hard to say it better than that. Although Rabbi Metzger said much the same thing that morning by his very presence.

Love,

Harold

March 4, 2002

Dear Harold,

I had trouble finding the house. I veered off Centre Street in New-ton, then down another side street, just as the directions said. All I could see were other houses. I knocked on the door of one, to ask where the synagogue was. It was next door all along. Not that you would know it, since except for the tiny sign out front that I missed, it looks like every other house on the block.

I ascended the steps to the door, still wondering if this really was the synagogue, when I found myself in what looked very much like a living room. There were bookcases at one end, a big table in the middle, and a pic-ture window overlooking the other Orthodox synagogue, the one that's easy to find but that I wasn't looking for that morning. Beyond the living room was what appeared to be a kitchen, and a woman sitting behind the counter who appeared to be the secretary.

"Rabbi Samuels will be ready in a few minutes."

I continued to wait, my eyes taking in this 1960s ranch house, conjur-ing up images of what the sanctuary must look like. Wondering if Rabbi Samuels was going to accept me. If he would believe that this girl from the Illinois farm who'd been a church organist and choir director for years was serious.

My thoughts darted across decades. How did I get here? What amaz-ing turns of fate brought me from that Illinois farm to the church choir loft to this living room? If my parents saw me now. If my friends from Farm-ington saw me now. If Pastor Bill at Colonial Hills Church saw me now. What would they say? That they're concerned for my soul – or that they're not surprised? What if . . .

"Hello, Gayle."

He had an engaging smile and seemed genuinely happy to see me. I followed Rabbi Samuels into his office, which I think had been a child's bedroom in the house's previous life. I settled into the chair, feeling waves of relief that this long process was finally to begin, and feeling waves of trepidation that this long process was finally to begin. The tiny space held what seemed like more books than the entire Farmington Public Library. Definitely more in Hebrew, anyway.

And I began. Growing up on the farm. Church every Sunday. Evangelical turn in college. Minister of Music at a Texas mega-church. Meeting you. Our Jewish experiences. Micah. Your turn toward Orthodoxy. My drift from Christianity. And so it went.

I have no idea how much time passed. But slowly, my monologue became a conversation. Rabbi Samuels smiled. He was positive, even encouraging. We talked about how I might gradually move from the church work to something more suitable for an Orthodox Jew. He said he would speak with the Beit Din to see how my singing might be synthesized with an observant Jewish life, given that it's part of my livelihood. He told me that what I was doing was great. I know a rabbi is supposed to turn away a potential convert three times to test her sincerity. But I had the feeling Rabbi Samuels has heard the stories of many potential converts and has a pretty good sense of their readiness.

At the end, he showed me the sanctuary, which thankfully does not resemble the rest of the house's décor. And he asked which books I've been reading. Hayim Halevy Donin's "To Be a Jew" – good. Aryeh Kaplan's translation of the Torah – good. Maurice Lamm's "Becoming a Jew" – good. Geza Vermes' "The Many Faces of Jesus" – that, he said, we could come back to for the graduate seminar – his polite way of telling me it was time to focus on Judaism rather than critiquing Christianity.

Then, in a gesture that validated everything I've been feeling these many months, he said, "I can really sense your sincerity."

In a way, though, he did turn me away, although not in the conventional sense. He said you and I have to consider which community we want to settle in, and that house prices in Newton are expensive. He asked me to speak with a few other rabbis in other communities to look into the possibility of converting there, and with Josh Jacobson, a conductor in his congregation, to discuss the musical life of an Orthodox Jew.

So in the end, I have a lot of additions to my book list, and a few new people to talk to. But it doesn't seem that I'm officially starting my conversion studies yet. It's not clear to me whether I must study with a rabbi in the community where we choose to settle and could study with Rabbi Samuels only if we move to Newton. It wouldn't be fair to take up so much of his time if we were going to wind up in some other congregation. And although I think Rabbi Samuels would be ideal, I ought to speak with a few others before I leap into this. I guess I'll start setting up those meetings.

Love,

Gayle

ॐ

March 11, 2002

Dear Gayle,

As one door begins to open, the time has finally come to close another. My heart and head (yours too) have been out of Temple Shalom for some time. Now that the Search Committee's work is coming to a close, we can move on. I'm tiring of shuttling between these two very different worlds. And in case I had any question about which world I belong in, the last round of interviews knocked me over the head with the answer.

After interviewing the Reform rabbi, the Reconstructionist rabbi, the Conservative rabbi, the Renewal rabbi and the unaffiliated rabbi, we interviewed an Orthodox rabbi. Rabbi Kornspan was ordained at Yeshiva University, but has been leading a traditional-leaning Conservative synagogue in the Midwest for twenty years. He's personable, experienced at working with a wide range of Jews, and more knowledgeable by far than any of our other candidates.

The interview started off well enough. At first, the younger committee members liked his answers to their questions, which were mostly about welcoming intermarried families and making the service shorter.

But the trouble began at the Shabbat morning service, when the rabbi had the audacity to perform a Jewish ritual in the synagogue. To speed up the transition between the service and the lunch, the Committee had decided that the rabbi should recite the blessing over the bread from where he stood in the sanctuary rather than right before the meal in the social hall. Of course, Jews traditionally wash their hands before saying the blessing.

So now Rabbi Kornspan is stuck up front holding two big challahs with no water in sight. He motioned to me, politely requested a bowl and pitcher, and then proceeded to wash his hands. Big mistake.

With their antennae now up, several search committee members grilled him during the lunch about how he planned to make Judaism compatible with such burning issues of modern life as Saturday morning sports leagues. They were none too impressed when he based his answers on Jewish sources like the Talmud and Maimonides.

Then came the committee meeting to discuss the rabbi's candidacy. One dour face after another opined that the rabbi is out of touch with today's young Jews, is anti-feminist, and apparently stands against the entire modern world.

Since I wouldn't have gotten very far had I said that their bogus objections were really about their own Jewish hang-ups, I chose instead to politely highlight the rabbi's many good qualities.

This proved too much for one of the synagogue officers, who cut me off abruptly, half-shouting, "We are not a handwashing congregation!" Yes, everyone agreed – wasn't it just terrible that he made such a public display of washing his hands? He says he's a Conservative rabbi, but we all know he's a closet Orthodox rabbi. And if he comes here, he'll try to make all of us Orthodox.

And on and on it went. I walked out knowing that, even if we wanted to stay, there is no way to grow here. I am already the freak who walks to synagogue on Shabbat. The Education Director let slip that a few whispers are passing around the congregation that we've joined a cult – the reason being that we're sending our son to a Chabad pre-school. It's irrelevant that Shaloh House is a great pre-school, or that a Conservative rabbi is also sending her child there. It's Chabad and it's Orthodox – so the only explanation is that we've been brainwashed. The parents who are sending their kids to secular pre-schools, to eat ham and cheese sandwiches and learn nothing about Judaism – they're normal.

So yes, please speak to the other rabbis that Rabbi Samuels mentioned – and then we can decide which handwashing congregation we want to join.

Love,

Harold

৵৵

March 12, 2002

Dear Harold,

It's been quite a road trip. When we began to look for a synagogue, I thought there was no way we could go beyond Reform. But unable to find a Reform temple where the cantor didn't make me cringe each time he opened his mouth, I suggested we just try the place nearest to us. Knowing it was Conservative, we both walked through Temple Shalom's doors with more than a little angst. You didn't think you could handle the Hebrew, and I wasn't sure if I could handle any of it.

Despite it being a foreign world for both of us, we stayed because the Cantor was good, the people were friendly, and Rabbi Fogel encouraged my involvement without the need to convert.

Here we are, just a couple of years later, and I'm running around meeting with Orthodox rabbis. Read a few books, start carving out time on Saturdays, make a few dietary changes, and all of a sudden, this intermarried family is a candidate for Orthodox cult membership – at least according to certain Conservative congregants.

I entered Temple Shalom as a Christian woman wondering if I could handle all of the tradition, and how I would adjust to such a heavily Jewish atmosphere. I leave Temple Shalom as an Orthodox convert-to-be, wondering why so few of the parents are serious about introducing their children to Jewish life, disappointed that Micah is one of the only kids at Shabbat services, and discovering my best learning and spiritual experiences in the Orthodox world.

Okay, so there are still a few issues to work out, like finding something to replace that church organist/choir director job I'm holding. But we'll get there – of that, I have no doubt.

Did they really have a problem with the rabbi washing his hands? Yes, time to move on. The Cantor is leaving in a few months anyway.

Love,

Gayle

ॐॐ

March 21, 2002

Dear Harold,

With just a week to go until Passover, the only mention it receives at United Church is in connection with Jesus' last supper. Seven miles away at Shaloh House Pre-School, the outlook on Passover is rather different.

You should have seen Micah when I picked him up today. He had decided to become Pharaoh. There he sat on his throne. I mistakenly thought he was sitting in the cubbies where the kids hang up their coats. No, he assured me – these are not cubbies – this is Pharaoh's throne. Over and over, he said, "No, no, no, I will not let them go!" as children reached around him to grab their coats. He loves the teachers, the kids, and everything he is learning. And I sense that they love him just as much.

I was pretty reluctant when you first mentioned this place, especially since it was at a time when the road ahead was not so clear. I was sure I would feel ill at ease sending my child to a school where the rabbi looks straight out of central casting for Fiddler on the Roof. *At the time, I would have gladly considered almost any other option – except that, strangely enough, this Chabad pre-school was the only one that could accommodate my schedule working at a church and teaching at an Evangelical Christian college. Now, it's a haven for Micah, and I couldn't imagine him anywhere else.*

Even though I'm now beginning the conversion process, I'm still afraid that they'll discover I'm not Jewish. There are other non-Jewish spouses who send their children to this very Orthodox pre-school. It's just that we never actually told them our situation. Although, I have a feeling it wouldn't matter to any of the teachers, or even to the rabbi.

When he's not busy playing Pharaoh on his cubby-hole throne, Micah readily connects with the character of Moses. He was adorable when we had three feet of snow a few weeks ago – watching him clamber up a huge mound of snow, lift a large, crusty piece of ice and slam it down on the (freshly shoveled) driveway, proclaiming, "I'm throwing down the tablets because the people forgot about God!"

There's something so innocent in his childlike faith – I know I'm too sentimental, but the tears begin to flow whenever I think about it. The good people at Shaloh House understand that faith, and nurture it. Even as we deal with the very real frustrations of the adult world, we need to keep nurturing that faith in him – and in ourselves. I realize how much he needs us, and how much blessing his presence has brought us.

In the meantime, back at United Church, Easter's coming up and I need to prepare the music.

Love,

Gayle

৵৽

May 15, 2002

Dear Gayle,

I'm in sticker shock. Kosher food can be had without much additional expense, especially if we're creative. Books about Judaism cost no more than books about anything else. Most of the classes we attend are free.

Then there's tefillin. Those little black boxes with the leather straps that wrap around the arm and head during weekday morning prayer, fulfilling the verses immediately following the Shema in the book of Deuteronomy: "And you shall bind these words as a sign on your hand and as a symbol between your eyes." Tefillin offer a good example of how what's come to be known as the Oral

Law (codified in the Mishna around the year 200) complements the Written Law in the Torah. So often, as here, the Torah tells us what to do, but omits any details about how to do it. The Oral Law supplies those details.

Evidence of tefillin is quite ancient – they even discovered some alongside the Dead Sea Scrolls in the Judean desert, used by the Essene Sect at least 2,100 years ago. The Essene version has four compartments, one each for four verses from the Torah, just as tefillin do today.

I have a feeling the Essenes got their tefillin for a lot less. Today's version can cost hundreds of dollars, or more. The leather straps, the boxes and the parchment are made from kosher animals and often assembled by hand. Each letter on the four tiny scrolls is painstakingly inscribed by the hand of a trained scribe, using a special pen and ink.

Despite the labor-intensiveness, it still seems like a lot of money. Then again, people unthinkingly plunk down far more for a mass-produced television that they'll replace in a few years.

To buy a pair of tefillin requires only a credit card. To use them is a bit more daunting. One of the straps is wound around the arm seven times, representing the seven days of the week. Then three times around the middle finger as a kind of wedding ring to God, and on up around the hand in a pattern whose intricacy makes me long for the knot-tying tests of my Boy Scout days.

I tried learning it from a book, but quickly determined I required outside assistance. Rabbi Gurkow at Shaloh House was kind enough to take me through the process several times.

Only, none of it stuck. I was too embarrassed to go back to Rabbi Gurkow. So I tried Rabbi Glaser at Aish, pretending like this was the first time. Rabbi Glaser spent an hour with me, showing more patience than I have with myself as the tefillin straps dangled in every direction. But this time, I wrote everything down, step by step, in minute detail. I suppose someone who is mechanically inclined wouldn't sweat this. But for someone like me, who takes hours to put together items marked "Easy to assemble – only takes a few minutes," tefillin presents something of a challenge.

Strangely, once I manage to put the tefillin on correctly, something special happens. I can't describe it, other than to say there's some bit of extra focus as I'm praying that doesn't feel like it's coming from me.

Just like keeping kosher, tefillin make no rational sense. But it does make sense – only, there's no way to explain it.

Love,

Harold

ॐ✎

June 23, 2002

Dear Harold,

Finally, staying with the Jacobsons in Newton, it felt like we were "doing Shabbat" the way it's supposed to be done. An entire 25 hours without the phone ringing or the news blaring. We've tried to do this at home, but it's not the same when we live miles from the closest synagogue. We also did Shabbat at the Homawack Hotel, but it makes a difference when you take the musty shag carpeting out of the equation.

To see Josh Jacobson the musician happily co-exist with Josh Jacobson the Orthodox Jew gives me hope that I'll also find a way to bring these two worlds together. And I learned a lot about the practical aspects of Shabbat watching his wife, Ronda – everything from how to prepare mountains of food in advance of Friday evening to the "choreography" of having many and diverse guests over for the meals.

I'm constantly amazed how, for observant Jews, these otherwise mundane details effortlessly meld with the spiritual. When I hadn't brought my hat downstairs, Ronda asked me if I'd like something to cover my hair before lighting candles. The way she asked, there was no feeling of pressure, no hint of condescension, just someone who sincerely wanted to help. She then waited in the next room while I lit candles with Micah, to make sure I had time to complete any prayers I might want to say.

What I was thinking, though, as the flames blossomed up from the wicks, was whether it's right for me to be doing this, and whether Ronda knows that my conversion hasn't happened yet. These situations are beginning to feel awkward – I don't want to present myself as something I'm not, but I don't feel the need to announce my status to the world every time I enter a new setting.

Sometimes I get discouraged by how much I still have to learn. I know that observant Jews "bench" after the meal, saying and sometimes singing a beautiful prayer of thanks to God, fulfilling the verse in Deuteronomy, "When you have eaten and are satisfied, bless the Lord for the good land which he has given you."

But knowing why things are done is not the same as doing them. When everyone around the table started singing the blessings using tunes I had never heard and at a pace well beyond that of my beginning Hebrew class, I just sank down in my chair a little, hoping nobody would see my lips not moving behind a maze of Hebrew words. Although I noticed you weren't exactly participating either. I guess we both have a lot to learn.

Just like Kadima-Toras Moshe, the people at Congregation Shaarei Tefillah are not only friendly, but genuine. That made it all the more depressing to hear how expensive houses are in Newton. Several long-timers told me they couldn't afford their homes if they were to move to Newton today. I love the area, the people, and of course Rabbi Samuels. But I don't know how we could ever afford it. And the area around Kadima-Toras Moshe and Young Israel is even more expensive.

Meanwhile, Samantha, who seems to be Shaarei Tefillah's de facto real estate agent, is still working on finding something we can afford. If nothing else, Samantha has allayed my fears that to dress modestly as Orthodox women do, is to resign oneself to looking frumpy. For Samantha, modesty has become a fashion statement. I don't think she found her feathery black hat and matching suit at Target.

Love,

Gayle

࿐

September 24, 2002

Dear Gayle,

From our window, I am witnessing an upside-down sukkah blowing around our neighbor's yard just steps away from their statue of the virgin Mary. The nice people from Israel Book Shop who sold us the sukkah neglected to mention that the "lightweight" interlocking poles need extra weight on top to keep the edifice from blowing over in the face of strong winds such as we had last night.

They also neglected to mention that when living in a predominantly Irish Catholic neighborhood, such an occurrence can cause grave embarrassment. The holiday of Sukkot is not a household word even among many Jews, never mind the general population. I can say with confidence that we are the only family with a sukkah on our block – or the next block, or the one after that. Even when our sukkah stood upright, I cannot imagine it escaped the notice of our neighbors. No one said anything, even as they saw us carry our meals out to it.

Perhaps they were just being polite. Perhaps they were curious, but didn't know quite how to broach the subject. "Excuse me, but I happened to notice that you put up a tent in your yard a few days ago – well not exactly a tent, but kind of a thing with, well, they look like corn husks on the roof. What in the world is . . . what I mean to say is . . ."

Yes, our neighbors are nice people, and they couldn't think of a polite way to ask. When we were the only ones without Christmas decorations, they could ignore that. And even when this hut suddenly appeared but was in OUR yard, they could write it off as some quirky but benign development. This morning, however, it sits in THEIR yard, threatening to invade the domain of the virgin Mary herself.

There must be some deep symbolism in this, but all I can do right now is laugh uncontrollably every time I peer out the window.

I think I'll go out, though, and move it back to its place. And put a lot more weight on top.

Love,

Harold

∂∽∾

December 16, 2002

Dear Harold,

We managed to escape neighborly interrogation during Sukkot, despite the near collision with the virgin Mary. With Christmas approaching, however, our luck has run out.

I picked up Micah from Sally's house this afternoon. When I first discovered that Sally runs daycare in her home just up the street for when I need to teach a few hours of music lessons, I was thrilled. But if Micah's behavior continues as it's been, he may no longer be welcome.

Sally came out to see me even before I had reached her front door. With a look of great concern, she told me how Micah had devastated one of the girls. The girl was telling everyone what she thought Santa was going to bring her for Christmas. Micah unapologetically informed her that Santa does not exist. She was sure Micah was mistaken. But when Micah continued to insist that Santa was a figment of her imagination, she was beside herself.

Apparently, Sally then frantically showed Micah half a dozen photos of Santa to convince him that St. Nick is a real person after all. Micah looked at the photos, then looked up at Sally, and flatly proclaimed, "Fake."

Sally said that Micah can't come any more if he's going to ruin the other children's Christmas. Sally has been very accommodating, only feeding Micah the kosher food that I send. But I guess a line has to be drawn when it comes to Santa Claus.

I've been busy speaking with rabbis in several communities, and it's clear to me that we need to choose one soon – before Micah tells everyone that the Easter Bunny isn't real either.

Love,

Gayle

☙☙

Dear Harold,

I discovered an Orthodox community in a town we may be able to afford. It all came from the "Mommy and Me" poster you saw a few weeks ago at the Israel Book Shop – coincidentally, the wife of the administrator at Aish teaches the classes. Lori is so sweet and so positive with the children. She told me that there's a nice community in Malden and that she and her husband will soon be moving there. With the price of homes in Newton and Brookline, we should look into Malden. It would be nice to find a way to be within walking distance of an Orthodox synagogue without breaking the bank.

I also have to admit that I'm not in love with the mechitza at Ka-dimah-Toras Moshe. I don't mind the men and women being separated, and I agree it can lead to greater concentration during the prayers. In fact, I've come to appreciate the feeling of camaraderie and the close friendships that have developed as a result of praying only with the women, something that wouldn't be so easily achieved with mixed seating.

Nevertheless, some mechitzas are female-friendly, and some were so obviously designed by men who never gave a moment's thought to the women on the other side. I'd like to find a synagogue where I at least can see if Micah is with you or if I need to go on a scavenger hunt to find him.

In the meantime, Micah loves "Mommy and Me," probably because the other kids are as active as he is. But each time they start singing Jewish songs, I feel so stupid, being a singer and not being able to sing because I don't know the tunes or the words. Then comes snack time, which makes me feel more stupid. All of the other mothers instinctively tell their children which blessing to say on which kind of food. I'm still learning all of this, so I listen very carefully, and then, as confidently as I can, tell Micah what he should say. Fortunately, he's learned some of this already at Shaloh House, and so can often get by just fine without me.

If the other mothers have discovered that I'm not the product of a yeshiva education, they aren't letting on – everyone is as friendly as can be. Still, it amazes me how all of these details are so second-nature to these women. I guess they've been involved in Judaism just a bit longer than I have.

Love,

Gayle

ॐ✍

January 15, 2003

Dear Gayle,

Don't feel bad – I also missed that yeshiva education, so most of this is new to me too.

I'd love to check out Malden, or the couple of other lower-cost Orthodox alternatives. When I first learned that becoming Orthodox meant we would need to move, I didn't understand. But now I do.

Even if we didn't have to contend with an errant-blowing su-kkah or Micah disabusing young children of their cherished ideas about Santa, I've come to realize that being an observant Jew only works in the context of community. That is both the challenge and the beauty of it.

The need for community became especially clear when we stayed at the Jacobsons for Shabbat. "It takes a village . . ." could be the Torah's motto. There's plenty of room (and need) for the individual and for private spirituality. But living the Torah works only in tandem with others. Besides being able to walk to a synagogue on Shabbat, everything from communal prayer to Shabbat meals to caring for the sick to comforting the mourner to educating children presupposes a community.

My first feelings of being pulled toward the Torah were as an individual. But as I've grown into it, the communal becomes increasingly important. I admire how an Orthodox community functions as a community – people have their differences, and some of the same petty and not-so-petty issues exist there as elsewhere. But in the end, people care for each other, people help each other, people are there for each other. Because that's how the Torah is designed to work.

Love,

Harold

ॐ∞ॐ

February 6, 2003

Dear Harold,

I met again with Rabbi Samuels. Finally, I'm going to start for real!
After speaking with half a dozen rabbis, I'm still not sure which community is right for us. Rabbi Sendor in Sharon offered me encouragement. Rabbi Rabinowitz in Malden offered me a blessing. Rabbi Halbfinger at Kadimah-Toras Moshe offered me the third degree, but in a bizarre twist, ended our meeting by giving me the information for the Boston Beit Din and suggesting I submit my application.

I could see myself studying for conversion with several of the rabbis. But I started with Rabbi Samuels and feel most comfortable with him. He said I can begin as long as we continue our search for a community, even if it isn't Newton. He also made it clear that I won't be able to complete the conversion until we have settled in an Orthodox community.

I left the meeting feeling relieved that I'm at long last moving forward. I also left with a very long list of books Rabbi Samuels would like me to read. With a few thousand pages in front of me, the book I grabbed first was Spice and Spirit, *a kosher cookbook with a great introduction about keeping kosher and setting up a kosher kitchen. Great recipes, too. Before I get too far into this, we may want to buy stock in Barnes & Noble.*

Rabbi Samuels is guiding me through the application for the Boston Beit Din, which is the Rabbinical court through which all Boston-based candidates for Orthodox conversion must pass. The application is a volume in itself. He's already spoken with them about me, and it sounds like they're reasonable. I just wish there was some kind of checklist, so I would know what to do in what order and how long it would take. I'm not sure the rabbis realize that by the time someone has gone through the long process of making this life-altering decision, they would appreciate something more tangible than "we'll let you know when we think you're ready."

Hopefully, I'll have a better idea once I get a meeting with the Beit Din. In the meantime, I've made appointments with realtors in Malden and a couple of other communities. I think we should look for a house with built-in bookshelves.

Love,

Gayle

తుళ్

March 11, 2003

Dear Harold,

As hard as I'm working to become a Jew, can someone explain to me why some born Jews seem incapable of moving one inch in their observance? Everyone has to make their own choices. Yet I find it puzzling when some Jews react so aggressively against practices which have been part of Judaism for millennia.

Last night, at the informational meeting for prospective parents of the Maimonides Day School, many of the parents (all Jews) couldn't get past the observance issues that might come up if they were to send their children to this "too much" of an Orthodox day school. Even the parents who hosted the evening said they feared that if their children went to Maimonides, they might come home and "force" the family to be more religious.

After ten minutes of this, I found myself getting annoyed, and blurted out, "What are you afraid of?"

Well, they said, if there's a good game on television on Shabbat afternoon, they don't want to feel guilty about watching it. If there's a good vegetarian restaurant not supervised by a rabbi and not certified as kosher, they don't want to feel guilty about eating in it. Or if they want to end Shabbat a little early so they can go to a good concert, they don't want their children to make them feel like they didn't fully observe Shabbat.

As if it's so difficult to record a game and watch it later, eat in a different restaurant, or go to concerts any other time during the week or on a Saturday night during the majority of the year when Shabbat ends early enough. Ironically, this same host family commented that they don't drive on Shabbat and walked their daughter through the snow one Saturday afternoon so she could attend a classmate's birthday party.

They missed the fact that if their daughter were at an Orthodox day school, they wouldn't need to trudge through the snow because her classmates wouldn't be having their birthday parties on Shabbat. Yet they are quibbling over little things that take far less effort.

Then I thought about this path I'm on that has taken me from a Texas mega-church to a meeting about an Orthodox Jewish day school for our son. As a singer who will be an Orthodox Jew, I won't be performing on Friday nights and many Saturday nights. Then there is the issue that many Orthodox men won't listen to a woman sing, which could cut my Jewish audiences in half. I have a hard time sympathizing with people who can't give up attending a concert or two, or might need to leave the office a few minutes early on Friday afternoon should their child "force" them to become more observant.

Why do some Jews so passionately resist becoming more observant? They want their children to obey the rules about drugs, about extramarital affairs, even the traffic rules. But when it comes to Judaism, suddenly it's all about bending the rules when they become slightly inconvenient. What kind of message are they sending?

These parents claim their children will ultimately decide how much observance they will take on. But the parents have already decided for *them – this much and no further. They don't want their children to observe more than they do, so they won't feel guilty about what they're not doing.*

If I'm becoming a Jew, and we are raising our son as a Jew, then I want our son to know and experience everything Judaism has to offer, so he can make an informed choice when he grows up. The "this much and no further" approach would rob Micah of choices, limiting him to a Judaism that espouses observance, but whose highest value really is convenience.

I want Micah to grow up knowing what it means to be fully involved in Jewish life, to know what Judaism has to say about important issues, and to be able to pray as Jews have for centuries. When Micah is ready to start school, I want him to go to Maimonides.

Love,

Gayle

৵৶

March 13, 2003

Dear Gayle,

They're afraid of giving up their individuality and their freedom. They think that if they follow the Torah's commandments *in toto*, they will surrender a part of themselves they may not be able to reclaim. By holding back – leaving some wiggle room on Shabbat, or going to the restaurant that's almost, but not quite, kosher, or whatever – they feel like they're still in control.

This approach is quite common. But it reflects a complete misreading of what it means to observe the mitzvot. The mitzvot are not about giving up one's individuality, but about finding one's true path.

I've often thought that this is not unlike what I experienced during my clarinet-playing days. One hundred clarinetists will perform the Mozart Clarinet Concerto and each play exactly the same notes. But within those parameters, everyone will play it differently, according to their individual personality, their understanding of the music, and their abilities. Each player will take the same notes and make it their own. The confines of the notes become the vehicle for self-expression. As Igor Stravinsky put it, "The more constraints one imposes, the more one frees one's self."

If clarinetists approached Mozart the way some Jews approach Judaism, then instead of 100 clarinetists playing the same notes differently, some would decide they like part of Mozart's masterpiece, but take issue with how he wrote certain sections. They would then start changing notes here and there to conform to their personal preferences. If they changed a few notes, their rendition would be largely recognizable, but no longer true to Mozart's intent. If they changed enough of the notes, it might be Mozart-inspired – but it wouldn't be Mozart anymore, no matter how adamantly they might insist it is.

The Torah is vast, and many Jews, legitimately, do not feel equipped to observe all of the mitzvot all at once. Franz Rosenzweig, when he was first discovering Judaism, was asked if he put on tefillin. He replied, "not yet."

There is a vast gulf between "this much, and no further" and "not yet." "Not yet" offers the possibility of growth, of tomorrow holding the potential for greatness. "This much, and no further" offers a stagnant Judaism, of tomorrow offering no more than today. Jewish law is called "halachah" for a reason. Halachah comes from the Hebrew word meaning "to walk." To become an observant Jew is to follow a dynamic path, not to sit down somewhere in the middle, never to move again.

Love,

Harold

৵৽৵

May 18, 2003

Dear Harold,

Did you hear the joke about the church organist/choir director who is studying to become an Orthodox Jew, and who took her Jewish son to the church choir concert? I'm beginning to appreciate the line that truth is stranger than fiction.

I should have known better, but it seemed so harmless in the abstract. Micah loves music, so I thought he'd enjoy hearing the church choir concert. It's just music, not a service, so I thought to myself.

Little did I envision a four-year old boy walking up to everyone at the post-concert reception, demanding to know, "Is this food kosher?" While a gathering of Jews would answer that question with a simple yes or no, the church members were reduced to stunned silence.

Now that I'm officially "in training" to be a Jew, the time has finally come to resolve this part of my life. I keep waiting for a flash of inspiration, some magic moment when I'll think of an obvious professional alternative. But no great thoughts have come to me yet.

I suppose anything truly worthwhile requires giving up something to embrace something greater. I just wish I were living a life that made the giving up and embracing a bit less complicated.

Love,

Gayle

శ్రీఖ

May 19, 2003

Dear Gayle,

We are, so it seems, at an "in-between" point that's becoming more bizarre. I am reminded of this every Sunday morning.

Micah and I begin with an Orthodox daily morning service over at Shaloh House. Then, we're off to the Jewish Community Center for his swimming class, followed by bagels at the kosher bakery. And then, we usually drive past the white steeple of United Church just as services are letting out to meet up with you and run errands.

Few other families – Jewish, Christian, or even intermarried – fit this pattern. I'm not the one to tell you to make a leap. Only you can decide that. But when you decided it was time to leave Colonial Hills Church in Texas, Opera in the Schools landed in your lap just after you departed. Maybe it will take leaving Walpole for a suitable alternative to appear.

Love,

Harold

જ઼ન્જી

September 2, 2003

Dear Harold,

I came upon my appointment book for 1999, and for some reason started leafing through it. The entry for Friday, March 12 stared back at me. That was the day we made a dinner for your parents and my parents to tell them we had decided to adopt a child. We had no way of knowing that on that very day, in a city in northern Russia, that child was being born.

A coincidence, perhaps. But if so, then a very unusual one. What are the chances? Many adoptive parents say they feel it was meant to be that their child would be part of their family. For me, it's not a coincidence. It's not even strange that our child was born on the day we told our parents. Everything happened as it was supposed to happen.

The other night, I had a dream. A little girl in Russia was crying out, "Mama" and beckoning me to come to her. I woke up, unsure it was just a dream. Could it be that there is supposed to be a girl in our family?

I'd like to adopt again.

Love,

Gayle

જ઼ન્જી

September 3, 2003

Dear Gayle,

Just last week, Micah was asking me when he would have a sibling. Of course, he's thinking of a little brother. When I asked him what would happen if he woke up one morning and had a little sister, he said, "I guess I'd just have to put up with her." And so he will. Let's call the adoption agency.

Love,

Harold

☙❧

October 7, 2003

Dear Harold,

Do you remember that first Yom Kippur after I met you? As I sat in the Malden synagogue this year, my first Yom Kippur officially on the conversion path, I thought about how I fasted back then. I can't believe I did that. We had known each other only a few months, and I barely knew what Yom Kippur was.

I'm still fasting, of course. But everything else has changed. And all for the good, I think.

At the break-the-fast after services, I met Edy, a woman from Springfield whose family has ties to Malden and makes the two-hour trek every year for Yom Kippur. She described the area where she lives as a charming collection of Western Massachusetts neighborhoods with grassy medians and Victorian-era homes. It sounds very much like where we live now, except that it has an Orthodox community. If we can't find what we're looking for in the Boston area, maybe you can find a job in Springfield.

Love,

Gayle

෨෴

November 16, 2003

Dear Gayle,

This past Shabbat, in Malden, a young man read from the Torah. Not so unusual.

It wasn't even his Bar Mitzvah. Still not so unusual for someone who goes to a Jewish day school.

That is, until this young man's story comes out. His Bar
Mitzvah was last week. The Torah portion was *Lech Lecha*, in which
God tells Abraham, "Lech Lecha – Go forth." "Go forth, from your
land, from your birthplace, and from your father's house, to the
land that I will show you."

"Lech Lecha" also means "go to you," to yourself. Buried
within the Hebrew text is the momentous idea that in leaving his
geographic place of origin and "going forth," Abraham journeyed
inward to who he really was.

At his Bar Mitzvah, the young man spoke of this. He is a convert. He had entered the waters of the mikveh just a short time
before, along with his family. The congregation embraced him. Because his family didn't have the means for a party, the congregation
threw one for him.

And here he was, the next week, again called up to the Torah,
showing by example that the Bar Mitzvah is not the end, but the
beginning.

How could it be anything less for someone who has just
joined the Jewish people? For those who have been Jewish from
birth, it's too easy to reduce the Bar Mitzvah to a Jewish coming-
of-age event. I thought back to many other Bar Mitzvahs I've attended where the child reads from the Torah, has a big party, and
is never heard from again until Birthright, Hillel and Chabad go
chasing after them in college.

The last Bar Mitzvah I attended at Temple Shalom was for
a boy whose father is Jewish and mother is not. The boy appeared
self-conscious as he stumbled through his Torah portion. Then the

father spoke about how proud everyone was of him, thanked the Cantor for "getting him through" his Bar Mitzvah, and invited everyone to join them at the party at a nearby Irish pub that is most famous for its oysters on the half-shell.

I never saw that boy again. But here was this young man in Malden, coming back the following week, actively taking his place in the Jewish community.

I wish more born Jews would observe sincere converts. They could learn a lot about how to journey forth and find their Jewish selves in the process.

Love,

Harold

ॐ

Dear Harold,

From the time I learned to walk, I grew up hearing the stories of the Bible. Faraway places like Jerusalem, Jericho and Bethlehem became ingrained in my imagination – but it hadn't entered my thoughts that I would one day see these same names on road signs from a car window.

After a week of touring, Israel still felt a world away from our everyday lives, and yet somehow familiar. Everything here takes on special meaning, even in funny ways. Like on our first night in Jerusalem, when Micah spotted the Orthodox Union building from our hotel room, with the familiar OU symbol on the building's front that adorns the many products they certify as kosher. I couldn't stop laughing when Micah blurted out, "Look! That building is kosher!"

On the drive to the Dead Sea, I marveled at how a stark desert with hardly a plant in sight could be so beautiful. Looking at the swirling sand on the high hills overlooking the shore line, I thought back to Ruth and Naomi who came from these very hills, then known as the "hills of Moab." When I think of the courage it took for Ruth to leave the land she had known since birth to come to Israel and join the Jewish people, my own little journey seems less daunting.

Aside from visiting the Western Wall, the highlight of my trip was spending the day with Ahuvah Gray. After reading My Sister, the Jew, it was a privilege to meet her in person and talk one-on-one about the path from Christianity to Judaism. Since Ahuvah had been a minister, and now lives as an Orthodox Jew in Jerusalem, her experience gives me a lot of strength. She was so encouraging, and made me feel so positive about my decision. She also had some helpful suggestions for preparing for the Beit Din, and integrating music into my new life. Like Shana, she thought that the right opportunities would present themselves. I hope she's right. I also was encouraged to hear that, as a convert living in a very Orthodox community, she is so highly regarded and respected.

Then there was the Kotel – the Western Wall, also known for centuries as the Wailing Wall. All my life, I've heard about people visiting the "Wailing Wall." I approached with trepidation, not sure what I'd feel. What do other people feel? Is it like an electric shock, a warm embrace, a gentle rush of emotion?

As I stepped toward the wall, I felt repelled. For some reason, I was not ready to touch those ancient stones so near to where the Temple had stood. I wondered if it was because I'm not yet Jewish. No – people of all faiths pray at the Wall. Was it because I don't know the right prayers? No – people of all faiths say all kinds of prayers at the Wall.

Was it because I didn't feel quite ready to be enveloped by the thousands of years of history that are absorbed in this massive structure? I think that's it. I didn't feel prepared. I didn't feel worthy. As we had learned in Tzfat a few days before, the mystics who gathered there centuries ago didn't come into the world with all of that mysticism. It entered their souls through years of pondering the Torah and meditating on ancient texts, and praying fervently for understanding. I'm ready to return to Rabbi Samuels and do a lot more learning.

I couldn't believe our little four-year old in the car on the way to the airport. "Where are we going, Abba?" "Well, Micah, we're going home." "Abba, I don't want to go home!" "Why don't you want to go home, Micah?" "I want to stay here. I want to live in Israel so I can pray at the Kotel every day."

*Coming back to the U.S. hasn't diminished Micah's enthusiasm.
When I picked him up from Shaloh House this afternoon, the Director told
me that she was speaking with Micah earlier in the day, when he blurted
out, "I have to go back." The Director asked, "To the bathroom, or to your
classroom?" "No, to Israel. But first, I need to say goodbye to my friend,
Timmy."*

"When are you moving to Israel?" the Director asked.
"On Wednesday."

Love,

Gayle

ক৵৻৶

January 14, 2004

Dear Gayle,

Such a great spiritual sense in such a little body. Where does
it come from?

While you were struggling on your side of the Wall, Micah
was making bold requests of God from our side. Micah strode to
the front and began "writing" a prayer to place in one of the cracks
between the stones. Since, of course, Micah cannot yet write, he
scribbled on the paper, but clearly had something in mind beyond
his squiggles.

After Micah found an empty crevice just big enough for his
paper, I asked him what he had prayed for.

He replied, "I asked that everyone in the world should know
that God is one, and that there should be peace over Jerusalem."

What do you say when these sentiments come out of the
mouth of someone who hasn't yet entered kindergarten?

There's something indefinable about the Wall that elicits
such profound reactions. I think it is, as you say, that thousands of
years of history are concentrated in this one place. In these stones
reside centuries of yearning, thousands of tears, countless prayers.

Actually, I felt this indefinable something throughout Israel. It's hard not to sense, as you traverse its ancient pathways and super-modern highways, that you are experiencing a miracle of history.

In the midst of busy cities and lush forests, I recalled Mark Twain's words, confirmed by other travelers from his day, when he visited the Holy Land in 1867:

A desolate country whose soil is rich enough, but is given over wholly to weeds . . . a silent mournful expanse . . . a desolation . . . hardly a tree or shrub anywhere. Even the olive tree and the cactus, those fast friends of a worthless soil, had almost deserted the country.

Twain might be shocked to find a modern Israel that is a world leader in agriculture, high tech and medical science. Everywhere we went, I felt history almost shouting at me. The many centuries that Jews ended the Seder with "Next year in Jerusalem" even as persecution and expulsion loomed. It's impossible to imagine the sweep of Jewish history while walking the Jerusalem of today, and believe that there's nothing more transcendent here than happenstance.

On Jewish history too, Twain made his observations, which can hit you hard when traveling around modern Israel:

The Egyptian, the Babylonian, and the Persian rose, filled the planet with sound and splendor, then . . . passed away. The Greek and the Roman followed. The Jew saw them all, beat them all, and is now what he always was, exhibiting no decadence, no infirmities of age, no weakening of his parts ... All things are mortal but the Jew; all other forces pass, but he remains. What is the secret of his immortality?

Twain was not alone. Leo Tolstoy, John Adams, Winston Churchill, Blaise Pascal, and many others with no Jewish axe to grind said much the same thing.

None of this is a cause for undue pride, but rather for humility. Saadia Gaon, one of the great rabbis who lived about 1,000 years ago, provides an answer to Twain's parting question: "Our nation is only a nation by virtue of its Torah." As we move down this long road together, we are staking our claim to something vast, deep and incomprehensibly greater than ourselves.

Love,

Harold

ช่∘๙

February 18, 2004

Dear Harold,

I finally have a meeting with the Beit Din. I'm meeting with Rabbi Samuels tomorrow to begin preparing. All I can do is think about every possible question they might ask me. I have no idea what to expect.

Love,

Gayle

ช่∘๙

March 9, 2004

Dear Harold,

Now I understand why the Beit Din is considered a Rabbinical court – they made me feel like I was sitting in the defendant's seat, on trial for some unimaginable crime, reduced to beg for a more lenient sentence.

The crime, apparently, is that I want to become a Jew. I followed all of Rabbi Samuels' suggestions, dressed modestly, and prepared thoroughly. None of it seemed to matter.

One rabbi, in particular, fancied himself as the prosecuting attorney whose role was to cross-examine me. "How can you live the rest of your life and never again sing the Verdi "Requiem?" How can you never again sing the Mozart "Requiem?" How can you never again sing Handel's "Messiah?"

I explained that there is a lot of other wonderful music in the world without any connection to Christianity, and that I don't need to perform the music he mentioned to have a fulfilling musical life.

Whatever I said fell on deaf ears. He shot back, "I don't see the struggle in your application." (I told my entire story in my application. How do you "struggle" in an application, I wondered.)

"How do I know you're really serious about this?" (If he didn't notice the struggle in my application, perhaps he could have noticed the time period over which all of this has happened and realized that I didn't come to this overnight.)

"You've made such a difference in the lives of Christians with your music. You could still do so much more in the world!" (I wanted to scream, "have you even read my application where I addressed all of this? Have you even spoken with Rabbi Samuels? And why is Rabbi Samuels not saying anything? We've talked about all of these issues.")

Then this rabbi peered down at me from the "stage" on which they were sitting, leaned toward me, and with a sneer, shouted at me, "YOU DON'T HAVE TO CONVERT!"

Enough is enough! I leaned toward the rabbi and shouted back, "YES – I – DO!"

Then one of the other rabbis awoke from his silence, and suggested that, as my next assignment, I read "My Name is Asher Lev." In the story, Asher Lev is born into a Chasidic family and discovers he has an artistic gift. By the end of the story, he has painted a crucifixion scene with his mother in the painting. I'm still scratching my head and wondering how this relates to a musician who grew up on a farm in Central Illinois, has already chosen to become an Orthodox Jew, and has already stated emphatically that she has no problem performing all the other music in the world that is not Christian.

When I spoke with Rabbi Samuels afterward, he said that I need to try to see it from their perspective. And what perspective is that? If they had legitimate questions about my application, they could have asked me and listened to my answers rather than just shouting at me.

The "Asher Lev" recommendation convinces me that these rabbis have no clue about what my musical life entails, but have no problem making assumptions based on their lack of understanding.

Actually, one member of the Beit Din possesses a very keen under-standing. I was wondering how it came to be that the rabbi doing most of the shouting was asking me about very specific Christian pieces. They don't teach about the Verdi "Requiem" or Handel's "Messiah" in Rabbinical school. Where did he learn so much about Christian music?

I later heard that he had been a one-time singer, and gave it up when he became a rabbi. Now it all makes sense. He has his own issues to deal with, and my story pushed his buttons.

I believe that in a secular court, when a judge has issues that create even a suspicion that he cannot fairly judge the case, he must recuse himself. If this rabbi can't get beyond his own issues, then he should consider doing the same. I came to them to convert, not to be somebody's therapeutic punch-ing bag.

I know they have to turn me away three times. But I now know enough about Jewish sources to know that they don't need to act like this to turn me away. If a rabbi is not capable of treating someone with basic decency (as the Torah requires), perhaps he shouldn't sit on a Beit Din.

I love Judaism. Right now, I want nothing more than to become a Jew, and to have a Jewish family. But I hate this process.

Love,

Gayle

ॐ

March 10, 2004

Dear Gayle,

I cannot fathom why a Beit Din would feel the need to be so abusive. Rigorous – yes. Make sure you're sincere – of course. Turn you away at first – it's part of the process.

But they don't have to go out of their way to be nasty. You're right – treating someone like this is completely against Jewish law. And it's certainly contrary to the Jewish idea of Derech Eretz – just treating someone with basic courtesy.

I wonder if they have any idea how bad this makes them look – and by extension, Judaism. There's no excuse for anyone to act like that. But it's especially troubling when it comes from a rabbi. No amount of rigorous examination requires them to sink to such immaturity.

If they had read your application and spoken with Rabbi Samuels beforehand, then they knew all of the issues and still invited you to meet with them. So I must assume that, despite their crude theatrics, they at least envision the possibility of your conversion. Otherwise, why meet with you at all?

As emotionally draining as this must be right now (and needlessly so), you have to keep remembering that you have chosen a truly special path that has been trod by some very special souls before you. I've been reading about some of the amazing converts who have become an indispensable part of the Jewish people. Rabbi Hillel, whose opinions we follow to this day, was taught by Shmaya and Avtalyon – both converts. The great Rabbi Akiva – son of a convert. Onkelos, whose second-century translation of the Bible to Aramaic is part of all traditional Torah commentaries – a convert. And if the Beit Din is concerned about your church background, they should look at the scores of former Christian ministers in our own time who are now Orthodox Jews.

Nearly 1,000 years ago, the great Maimonides wrote a letter of consolation to Ovadiah, a convert who had been insulted by his teacher. Maimonides writes, "Your rabbi sinned seriously . . . It is appropriate for him to beg you for forgiveness . . . He should fast, cry and pray. . . . Even had he been correct and you wrong, he was obligated to be gentle."

Maimonides continues, "The obligation which the Torah places on us regarding converts is huge. We are commanded to honor and fear our parents, and to obey prophets. A person can honor, fear and obey, and not love. However, regarding converts, the Torah requires us to love with all the power that the heart has."

If this is the Beit Din's obligation to a convert, do they have no obligation to be gentle and loving to a fellow human being who approaches them and asks with complete sincerity to join the Jewish people?

Love,

Harold

ॐ

April 28, 2004

Dear Harold,

Not many people could interview to be the Director of the Spring-field Jewish Federation one week, and Director of the Wisconsin Conserv-atory of Music in Milwaukee the next. But you might just manage to pull it off.

In the meantime, you keep obsessing over whether a cross-country, or even a cross-state move is going to impact my conversion process. Just take the interviews and we'll see what happens.

As you know, I'm not a great fan of the Boston Beit Din anyway. A move might not be a bad thing. Springfield sounded so nice when that woman I met in Malden described it on Yom Kippur. And Milwaukee would be closer to my family.

Whatever happens, we'll make the right decision.

Love,

Gayle

ॐ

May 13, 2004

Dear Gayle,

The rabbis of old said that everything happens for a reason, and that we need to listen carefully to discern the message God is sending us. If we pay attention, the Sages say, we will understand that everything God does is for the good, and that the actions we take in response will carry us to the right place.

I have been listening carefully, and I think I know what God is trying to tell me. He wants me to know that He has a sense of humor. Granted, this doesn't seem very funny to me, but I imagine this must be a riot for Him.

Milwaukee called last night to offer me the job. Springfield called tonight to offer me the job. Anyone would say this is a great problem to have, but I'm now struggling to figure out in which world I belong.

I understand why God has given me these two choices – Judaism and the arts have been the two biggest forces in my life. But a bit more direction would be appreciated. So far, it seems all God is saying is, "It was nice of Me to offer you these two choices. Don't expect Me to make the decision for you, too. You're on your own." What a riot. Thanks a lot.

I've written out my usual list of pros and cons. Both are Director positions. The salaries are virtually identical. The cost of living is similar. Springfield is closer to my parents, while Milwaukee is closer to yours. They both have a good Jewish day school for Micah. They both have an Orthodox community.

This decision is not mine alone. More than salary or position, I have to know where you will be happy. I must admit that you haven't made this any easier. Every time I've broached the subject, you've said that each place has pluses and minuses, and you truly could be happy in either. Thanks a lot.

So in the end, it would seem God has sent me these two neatly wrapped packages so that I can choose how I want to focus my life. Thanks a lot.

What to do . . . I already discussed the observance issues with the Board Chair in Milwaukee. The Board is happy to make any necessary accommodations for Shabbat and the Holidays. And there's a kosher restaurant half a block from the Conservatory.

It almost sounds too good to be true. Before I could accept, I would need to make sure they really understand what they're getting themselves into.

Of course, I wouldn't have to worry about any of that in Springfield. There are no Federation events on Shabbat and Holidays. All the food is kosher. If anything, the Federation Director is supposed to be a Jewish role model for the community. At the interview, one of the Board members even asked me whether we would send Micah to the day school, and she clearly expected me to say yes.

Ah, the light bulb just went on.

They don't know that we're intermarried. They don't know that you are in the midst of converting. I didn't give it much thought before because, in my mind, we committed a long time ago to being a Jewish family. I can't remember when we last thought of ourselves as intermarried.

But we aren't a Jewish family quite yet. Communities don't have the same Jewish expectations of their Federation directors as they do of their rabbis. But I've never heard of an intermarried Federation director, and I'm pretty sure that that is not what Springfield thinks it is getting.

God must be laughing hysterically by now. Thanks a lot.

I can't take the job without telling them that I'm intermarried, just as I couldn't take the Conservatory job without telling them that I am observant. Nor am I willing to open this up for community discussion. All of Western Massachusetts does not need to know that we are not yet a Jewish family, but hope to become one soon.

I have to say something, though. Before I make any decisions, I need to meet with the Federation President, see if she can live with this, and can keep it confidential.

I can't read her well enough yet to know how she'll react. Did I mention that she is Orthodox?

Love,

Harold

৵৽

May 17, 2004

Dear Harold,

If the Board President is ok with our in-between status, then Springfield could be great for us. I drove out to Springfield this morning to meet with Rabbi Hyman. Rabbi Samuels had said he is a wonderful rabbi, and I have to agree. He might be an even better match for me than Rabbi Samuels, which is saying a lot.

We discussed my work so far with Rabbi Samuels, and Rabbi Hyman is happy to take me on as a student, should we come to Springfield. I can start studying with him upon arrival, and he will arrange for a Beit Din once he feels I'm ready.

In the afternoon, a realtor showed me around Forest Park, the Orthodox neighborhood. It is exactly as was described to me in Malden – huge Victorian homes set neatly on tree-lined streets. Nearby is the Jewish Community Center campus, with a day school just across the parking lot.

I'm ready to go to Springfield. I could also be happy in Milwaukee. But if you find yourself leaning in that direction, we would first need to fly out there so I could make sure there's a rabbi who will give me the same reception as Rabbi Hyman.

Love,

Gayle

꙳꙳

May 19, 2004

Dear Gayle,

The deed is done. This morning, as I sat in the Board President's dining room, with framed prints from Israel lining the walls, I told her that the person she has asked to be the Jewish Federation's next Executive Director is intermarried.

To my surprise, Ann was relieved. "When you called and said you needed to drive all the way out to Springfield to talk with me before you could take the job, my mind started to race. I thought it must be something big, that maybe you have some major medical problem that you need to disclose." Then, with a big smile, she said, "I'm so glad you're healthy."

It's good to know that our current situation pales in comparison to chronic disease.

I told Ann that this isn't an issue of interfaith marriage, but of timing. The question, I said, is whether she is comfortable with my becoming the Springfield Federation's Executive Director while still intermarried, knowing that we will be a Jewish family as soon as we can.

Ann took the situation in stride, far more than I did. As if people who are intermarried, but whose spouses are in the midst of converting, apply every day to run Jewish Federations. Perhaps this didn't seem like such an overwhelming issue once she learned I was not terminally ill.

Ann made very clear that they could not hire me if we were an intermarried family who planned to stay that way. Perhaps because we don't plan to stay that way, I feel very comfortable with the community's stance. A Jewish communal leader needs to be a Jewish role model, ideally in every respect.

Ann readily agreed that our situation would remain confidential, that to do otherwise would be an invasion of your privacy at this very sensitive moment in your life.

So this leaves me exactly where I started. Assuming there is an amenable rabbi in Milwaukee, I'm still looking at two paths, with nothing to tip the balance. Everyone is willing to accommodate me. I can be an Orthodox Jew in Milwaukee, or an intermarried one in Springfield.

I drove back to Boston, feeling pressured that everyone is expecting an answer from me, and I still don't know what it should be. I completed mile after monotonous mile of the Massachusetts Turnpike, imagining what each of the two roles would be like. As the traffic grew heavier, announcing that Boston was approaching, I pulled into a rest stop.

I sat quietly, I'm not sure for how long. Staring into the row of trees beyond the gas station, I made up my mind. There was no wrong decision here – only choices to be made. The net zero result of my pro and con list is exactly the point. We can live happily in either place. Whether my job is in the Jewish world or the arts, it will be possible to live rewarding Jewish lives.

A heaviness lifted away as I punched the numbers into the cell phone. At least I am getting on with it, I thought.

Important choices are uncomfortable. This would be no different.

"Hello," the Conservatory Board Chair's unsuspecting voice answered.

"Chris, this is Harold. I want you to know that I've really thought long and hard about all of our conversations. The Wisconsin Conservatory is a fabulous institution, and to be its Director is a great opportunity. It's just that . . . that . . . well, it's just that another position has been offered to me. I've been agonizing over this for days. It's been a very hard decision for me."

Silence on the line. I drew in a labored breath and forged ahead. "After a lot of reflection, I've decided to take the other position."

The Board Chair's disappointment resonated through the silent receiver. After a few seconds, he asked if I would be willing to think about it some more. Could they fly me out to Wisconsin to discuss it? Am I concerned about the Jewish observance issues, because they are committed to working around that.

No, I assured him, it is not the Jewish observance issues. I know how much they've been willing to accommodate me, and am very grateful. "I'm sorry," I said.

Love,

Harold

ৰ০৺

Dear Harold,

I have some job news, too. I didn't want to say anything until after we got through the Springfield/Milwaukee decision, because I didn't want this to muddy the waters.

Shana and Ahuvah were right – once you make the leap, everything starts to fall into place. Remember when we spent Shabbat with the Roth family in Sharon last month? Menucha and I hit it off from the start. Micah and her boys played so well together, unencumbered by all the electronic games that take over kids' lives on the weekdays. As we chatted, I thought about what a great friend Menucha could become.

My thought fell flat on its face when she announced they were moving to New Jersey this summer to be closer to her family. "Yes," she said, "I'm really going to miss all my friends here in Sharon, and I feel kind of guilty abandoning Arbah Kanfote."

My eyes widened and my ears perked up. I had gone to an Arbah Kanfote concert last year. They are the Boston area's Jewish women's chorus. "Arbah Kanfote" – the four corners – alludes to their repertoire of music from around the world. I remembered how much I enjoyed the concert and how well they performed.

"What do you mean, you are 'abandoning' them?" I asked. Menucha told me that when the founding director moved to Arizona last summer, Menucha stepped in since she played piano and could at least keep things going. But now, Menucha was leaving and they hadn't found anyone suitable to take her place.

"Menucha," I said, "Do you know what I do? I am a choral conductor and singer." She thought for a moment, and said, "But you live in Boston. Would you really want to travel all this distance?"

"Menucha, this could be a real blessing for me. What do I need to do?"

The rest, as they say, is history. I attended their final concert. I met with the group's leaders, who hired me immediately, and were thrilled that I would travel from Boston every week for the rehearsals.

I've now told them I'll be traveling from Springfield. It all works out – since I'll be keeping my college teaching position in Boston, and driving there once a week, I can just go to Sharon in the evening to run the rehearsal.

All this time I've been wondering what would replace the church choir, and now the perfect solution has dropped into my lap. The rabbi from the Boston Beit Din may be interested to know that no Verdi "Requiem" is required after all.

Maybe this is some sort of "sign" that everything is going to be ok with my music in my new life as a Jew. As they say, God works in mysterious ways. And you're right – I think He has a sense of humor.

Love,

Gayle

⤳⤶

October 14, 2004

Dear Harold,

Although the Springfield-Boston commute stretches to nearly two hours, it's worth it to keep teaching at Eastern Nazarene College, and of course to direct Arbah Kanfote. When I'm there, I'm not the wife of the Federation Director or the mother of a day school student. I'm just Gayle Berman.

If not for the teaching and performing, I would be spending all of my time dealing with the contractors for the house renovations, thinking about what we're going to have for dinner, and studying to become a Jew while appearing to the Springfield community as if I already am one.

Speaking of which – my meetings with Rabbi Hyman have picked up just where I left off with Rabbi Samuels. Every time I reach a new level of understanding, I discover how much more there is to learn. That's one of the things I like about becoming Jewish – no matter where I am, I can always reach higher.

In fact, for the past week I've been poring over a 400-page tome that Rabbi Hyman assigned, which covers every detail of Shabbat. I must *admit that I enjoyed the kosher cookbook a lot more, but I'm beginning to see Shabbat in a new way.*

Shabbat is so much more than a day of rest. It's a state of mind. It's a totally different way of relating to the world. The written Torah offers only basic details about Shabbat, not enough to observe it in any practical sense. As with so many of the Torah's mitzvot, we need the Oral Law to fill in the missing details. And those details come from an unlikely source – the Torah's instructions for building the Mishkan, or Tabernacle, in the desert.

To build the Mishkan, the Torah required many different functions, which can be divided into thirty-nine categories. In describing these functions, the Torah uses the Hebrew word "melacha," which is usually translated as "work." But that's not exactly what it means as we think of that word in English (for that, there's another Hebrew word, "avodah," which the Torah specifically does not use in this context).

The rabbis noted many parallels between the Torah's account of building the Mishkan and the Creation story. When God rests on Shabbat, as the culmination of Creation, the Torah specifically uses that same word –"melacha" – to describe the "work" from which God is resting:

"God finished all the work (melacha) that He had done. He ceased on the seventh day from all the work (melacha) that He had been doing."

Both the work/melacha of the Creation story and the work/melacha of building the Mishkan are not merely "work" in the mundane sense, but creative acts done for a higher purpose. Jewish thought even views the Mishkan as a microcosm of Creation and associates each part of the Mishkan with a corresponding act in the Creation story.

There are further parallels. To build the Mishkan, God appoints Bezalel, a man whom God has endowed with great artistic gifts. Just as God created the world, the Mishkan is not a mere building, but an act of creativity. And just as God created the world for us to live in, the Mishkan is intended to be a place for God to dwell (although, of course, He is everywhere).

Given both the linguistic and literary parallels between the accounts of Creation and the Mishkan, and that a discussion of Shabbat immediately follows the instructions for building the Mishkan in the Torah, Judaism identified the creative acts we refrain from doing on Shabbat as the same ones that were required to build the Mishkan. Just as God ceased from His week of creating for Shabbat, so we cease from our human creating – as associated with the Mishkan – to observe Shabbat. Just as God dwells in the Mishkan after we build it, so we "dwell" in Shabbat after our own week of creating.

There's a very important idea hidden behind all of the details – while the Torah regards the building of the Mishkan as our highest level of creativity, Shabbat transcends even our greatest creative acts. God didn't rest after the six days of Creation because He needed to lie down and take a nap. Rather, Shabbat became the pinnacle of Creation. While in the Torah, God calls all His other acts of Creation "good" or "very good," it is only Shabbat that he calls "holy."

All of this means far more than a "day of rest" as we typically think of it. Anyone can take any day of the week and lie on a beach. That's not Shabbat. Shabbat requires that we put up the conceptual fences of each melacha to block out the everyday world and create the space we need to tune in to what's truly important.

I can understand how, from the outside, all of the little details can seem like missing the forest for the trees. But the reality is the opposite. Without the trees, there's no forest. Without the details, there's no Shabbat. Each piece joins together to make up the whole, much like an intricate mosaic.

Of course, the spirit of Shabbat is important too. Because Shabbat is about refraining from creative activity, writing my name would violate Shabbat, while dragging a sofa around the living room technically wouldn't. But if I spent the day moving furniture just because no melacha is involved, I've missed the point of Shabbat.

Both the letter and the spirit of Shabbat are necessary. But the spirit doesn't exist in a vacuum. A person who does her own thing in her own way in her own time may feel good at first – but in the long run, that's not going to take her very far. The spirit can soar highest when it has a structure to hold it. I suppose that's what Judaism is all about.

Love,

Gayle

October 27, 2004

Dear Gayle,

Yes, one of the wonders of Judaism is that when all of these seemingly little details join forces, the spiritual depth is far beyond what we can see on the surface. I only wish more Jews could shed their baggage just long enough to experience how beautiful Judaism can be. Shabbat, prayer, Torah study, keeping kosher – these are not things to be feared, but to be enjoyed.

Yet, many Jews do fear Judaism – or at least the idea of being observant. Ironically, I've found many of the religious Christians I've met to be more respectful of my observance and have fewer issues with it than many Jews. But it's not so surprising – the Christians don't have any baggage. They can be respectful from a distance. Then again, it was not so long ago that I carried that baggage too. Everything happens in its own time, I suppose.

At Springfield's Heritage Academy Day School, I'm encountering this baggage almost daily in my Federation work. Several parents have told me that they'll only keep their children at the school through the early grades because they don't want them to become "too religious" and start requesting lifestyle changes in the home. A couple of parents have actually said they are taking their children out because they are intimidated that their children's Hebrew has surpassed their own.

I so much want to ask them the question you asked at the Maimonides School meeting – What are you afraid of? I cannot imagine a parent saying she is pulling her child from French class because the child's French has surpassed her own. If the child becomes fluent in French, the parent feels proud. But if the child's Hebrew, or observance, surpasses her own, then she feels inadequate. Clearly, something else is at play here. Deep down, she feels like she *should* know Hebrew, she *should* be doing these things that the child is learning about.

So wouldn't it just be easier to do these things instead of walking this psychological tightrope? Change is hard, and you hit the nail on the head with your question – under the surface, there's a great deal of fear involved. Fear of the unknown. Fear of losing their identity. Fear of buying into a system they don't yet understand. Fear of taking on new obligations. Fear that their friends, neighbors and relatives will think they've gone off the deep end and shun them. It's easier not to deal with the fear.

I want to assuage their fear, to tell them that it's ok, to ask that they consider taking a gentle first step on this path. Just try it, I want to say. What do you have to lose? What's the worst thing that could happen?

But I can't. As a Federation Director, I am walking my own tightrope – between my own convictions about what is spiritually true and my conviction that everyone must come to their own decisions in their own way, between my personal role as an observant Jew and my Federation role representing the wide range of Jews that comprise the community, between my observation that the Jewish people will get nowhere without a shared goal and the reality that shared goals by definition can only be embraced when people are ready.

The problem is that, as Jews, we have an aversion to shared goals, at least when there's no crisis looming. The story goes that a rabbi was giving a lecture at Aish a few years ago, discussing why the concept of Jewish unity is so elusive. When he joked to the group, "You know the old saying: two Jews, three opinions," a man in the back piped up, "Excuse me, rabbi, but I must correct you. I heard that it's supposed to be four Jews, five opinions."

Funny, but sadly, too true. We do a great job rallying together in the face of external threats. But we have a hard time figuring out who we are on the inside.

Maybe that's human nature. But in the meantime, at least from my little perch at the Federation, I see the Jewish people walking ever further along the tightrope. And not without some falling off.

Virtually every week, a member of the community comes to my office to discuss his own difficulties along the tightrope – the distraught grandfather whose grandson is being raised Catholic, the intermarried couple who is not practicing any religion and is meeting me only because the Jewish husband's parents insisted, the divorced dad who is trying to give his daughter a Jewish upbringing even as she lives most of the week with her Christian mother.

I'm not a miracle worker and I'm not a prophet. I have no magical solutions to offer. I can't even offer our own experience as an example, because the whole community thinks we are and always have been an Orthodox family. Maybe someday . . .

In the meantime, over at Heritage Academy, no one is happy with the tightrope. The observant families are clamoring for more Judaism in the school, while the less observant families are complaining that there's already too much.

I wonder if we'll ever learn to get out of our own way. Maybe someday . . .

Love,

Harold

ॐ⊶

November 8, 2004

Dear Harold,

As someone who was not born Jewish, I have a hard time relating to the idea of Judaism without Torah at the center. Unlike some born Jews, I can't connect to being Jewish just because my parents were Jewish, or I was brought up that way. I can't fall back on substituting a vague sense of Jewish culture or New Age spirituality for the mitzvot.

But Judaism isn't really about any of those things. God gave the Torah at Mount Sinai. Klezmer music, matzah ball soup and all other trappings of secular Jewish culture came later.

To be an observant Jew is a 24/7 program. You wake up in the morning and begin your first moments by saying the Modeh Ani, *thanking God for giving you another day of life. Then you recite a blessing after washing your hands, acknowledging that you should strive for your actions that day to be pure. Then you get dressed, wearing modest clothing because you are living a life where the physical should not distract from the workings of the mind and soul. Then you speak to God, saying the morning prayers. Then you recite blessings over your breakfast, which is kosher because even the food you put into your body matters.*

Then, as you go through your day, you strive to treat others as you wish to be treated, as the Torah requires. You strive to treat your family with all the love and respect the Torah requires. You speak to God again, saying the afternoon and evening prayers. At night, or whenever you have free time, you learn Torah, drawing on its wisdom to raise the level of every part of your life.

Some see this as burdensome. But it's what I've grown to love about Judaism. It matters – not twice a year or once a week or sometimes – but in every part of life. Judaism is not a possession that one holds dear whenever it's convenient, but discards whenever it's not. Judaism is a complete system that weaves its way into every activity. Practicing it this way makes you super-aware of where your thoughts are leading, what you are saying, what you are doing, and how you are treating others. By following all the details, you develop a keen sense of God's ongoing Presence – it's almost like having God next to you throughout the day.

Throughout all of the Torah, the word "religion" doesn't appear once. The concept, at least as Western culture understands it, is foreign to Judaism. The Torah describes an entire way of life, not merely a "religion."

Back to that Shabbat book I've been reading – I forgot to mention that Rabbi Hyman wants you to read it too. As he said, my conversion is not only about my becoming an observant Jew. Orthodox conversion requires that you also take on all of the mitzvot. I see great wisdom in this.

So much of Judaism takes place within the context of the family. The rabbis want to make sure that if I convert, I am living in a family that makes it possible for me to be an observant Jew.

So with that, I am pleased to bequeath to you these 400 pages of small print. Have fun.

Love,

Gayle

ॐ৵

January 31, 2005

Dear Gayle,

Five years later, Russia hasn't changed much. But we have.

Again, we're inside the Arctic Circle, shuttling from one Russian government office to another. Again, we're driving ever closer to a Russian orphanage, in this case the Regional Specialized Baby Home in the city of Apatity, a mere 100 miles from Micah's home town of Murmansk. Again, we're about to meet a certain young resident of the Baby Home, who is unaware that in just a few hours, her life – and ours – will change forever.

I think about how in the space between these two eerily similar trips, Micah has transformed from a Russian toddler to a boy with an overwhelming passion for all things Jewish. I wonder if Ilana will share that passion.

After her run-in with Santa, I kind of get the feeling she will. I was sitting in the orphanage director's office, waiting yet again on some paperwork. Ilana knew something big was about to happen. After the orphanage director had tried every possible way to get Ilana to stop wailing without a hint of success, I guess she thought the Santa figure on her shelf would do the trick. No kid can resist Santa, right?

Nothing doing. Ilana eyes Santa suspiciously, breaks into a scowl, folds her arms and turns her back on the little man with the red suit and white beard. The Jewish parent in me silently chuckles.

Finally, the paperwork arrives and it's time to go. As I pick up Ilana and carry her through the orphanage doorway to her new family, her new country, her new life, I start to wonder – is it really destiny, or simply blind chance, that she will grow up as an American Jewish child?

Again, I think back on the five years since we carried Micah through a similar orphanage doorway. The child who comes home each day from day school bursting with excitement, who asks to go to services with me, who asks question after question about what he sees there. The child who couldn't get enough of *Shalom Sesame* videos, and who at three began asking to visit Israel the way some kids clamor for Disneyworld.

Chance no longer seems like a viable option. These past five years with Micah have convinced me of the absolute truth of the Jewish belief that some souls stood at Sinai, even though they may not have been born into Jewish families.

And not only Micah. Five years ago, the only "Jewish" part of our trip was when you, as a Christian mother, explained to the court why and how Micah would be circumcised. This time, we enter Shabbat with a Jewish family at the U.S. Embassy Compound, go to services on Saturday morning at a Moscow synagogue, and have lunch with the rabbi's family – along with Jews from California, the East Coast, Israel, and several cities across Russia.

Five years later, I can no longer believe that we are simply adopting two children from Russia and raising them as Jews. Just as the Biblical Ruth described her conversion millennia ago, their souls are soon to become entwined with the God of Israel and the people of Israel. They, and we, are becoming part of something indescribably greater than ourselves.

I felt like we were living a miracle when we adopted Micah. I feel that way again. But experiencing a miracle is not enough. The real question is what we do with the miracle.

Anytime I want the answer to that question, I need only watch Micah, and Ilana, and you.

Love,

Harold

৵৽

February 2, 2005

Dear Harold,

I feel like we're part of a miracle too, but . . . the miracle hasn't been finalized. I'll feel much better once I'm on the other side of conversion. In the meantime, it feels like we're a Jewish family in every way – except that we're not yet a Jewish family.

That was driven home to me when Rabbi Perlman from the Jewish Community Center approached me just after we returned. "I hear you're planning on having the baby naming at the synagogue. We're all so excited for you. When is the baby naming going to be?"

"We'll have the Kiddush next Shabbat – lots of food – it'll be right after services," I replied. Throughout the conversation, he talked about the "baby naming" while I talked about the Kiddush.

There can't be a real baby naming until Ilana goes to the mikveh. And since Orthodox Judaism requires both parents to be Jewish to convert a child, that won't happen until I go to the mikveh. So in the meantime, we'll have a Kiddush celebrating Ilana's arrival, which most of the community will think is a celebration of the baby naming. When we get to the real baby naming, the community won't be invited because they will think that they celebrated the baby naming months before.

I'm not complaining – just pointing out that this double life we've chosen for ourselves may not have been the simplest way to become a Jewish family. I'll rest easier when we can just say we're a Jewish family – period.

Love,

Gayle

ক্ক

June 21, 2005

Dear Harold,

Finally!!
Rabbi Hyman says I'm ready. Now all that's left to do is that little matter of appearing before the three rabbis of the Beit Din, and convincing them to let me go for a dunk in the mikveh.

Since Springfield isn't exactly the center of American Jewish life, Rabbi Hyman wants to make sure that my conversion will be overseen by a Beit Din that everyone has heard of. He is now working with the Rabbinical

Council of America, of which he is a member. The RCA, as everyone calls it, is the largest Orthodox Rabbinical group in the country. They will authorize the Beit Din, which will operate under its auspices.

So all we're waiting for is the RCA to give the go-ahead. It shouldn't be long now.

Love,

Gayle

๛

September 26, 2005

Dear Gayle,

Any word yet from the RCA? I don't understand why they need three months to respond.

Love,

Harold

๛

September 27, 2005

Dear Harold,

Nothing yet. I've been told that setting a date is a simple matter, but that they are understaffed. Apparently they only review documents once a month, and if they don't get to your file, it gets bumped to the next month. Now that the High Holidays are coming up, I don't think they'll meet for a while.

Love,

Gayle

๛

December 20, 2005

Dear Gayle,

Still no word? In my line of work, I would be fired if I took six months to get back to people. When you first mentioned the RCA, I thought of the electronics company. But that RCA would have responded a long time ago.
Love,

Harold

❧

March 12, 2006

Dear Gayle,

Still no word?
Love,

Harold

❧

March 15, 2006

Dear Harold,

Still no word. At one time, the other RCA's slogan was "His Master's Voice." I'm beginning to feel like I'm just sitting here waiting for "His Master's Voice" to summon me. It would be nice to know how long the wait is going to be.
Love
Gayle

❧

July 26, 2006

Dear Harold,

Everything is different visiting Israel this time, especially the Kotel. This time, I had no feelings of being repelled or being unworthy. I stepped right up to the Wall and began to pray. My prayers were in Hebrew, the same ones Jews have been saying at the Wall forever. And I realized that they are now MY prayers. The prayers belong to me and I belong at the Kotel.

Just as soon as Rabbi Hyman hears from the RCA, whenever that may be, I can make it official. I can't wait.

Love,

Gayle

ॐॐ

September 15, 2006

Dear Harold,

I hope you're sitting down. The RCA came through. Yes, you read that correctly. Everything should happen in a month, right after the Holidays.
Love,

Gayle

ॐॐ

October 22, 2006 – Hebrew Date: 30 Tishrei 5767

Dear Harold,

It's Sunday morning. Growing up, Sunday morning meant going to church with my parents. When we met, Sunday morning meant getting through the music for three services at a mega-church. Even not so long ago, Sunday morning meant conducting the church choir and playing organ in Walpole.

This is not one of those Sunday mornings. I'm nervous as we get into the car together, distracting myself by asking if you took along the new transformer action figure for Micah and the doll for Ilana. I know they'll like them. Sometimes bribery can be more effective with children than the most well-reasoned explanations.

As we pull into the mikveh parking lot, panic overtakes me. Not for what's about to happen, but because we might be spotted. Everyone drives by here. They'll see our car. They'll wonder why, since women make their monthly trip to the mikveh at night, our car is sitting here on a Sunday morning.

Deep breath. I can't worry about any of that now.

As you take Micah and Ilana to another room, Tova flashes me her warm smile and embraces me. I realize how much Tova has been an anchor for me. Ever since I began studying with Rabbi Hyman, I always knew I could call Tova about anything, ask her questions about anything, confide in her about anything. As important as Rabbi Hyman has been, I now see how much responsibility for the community sits on the shoulders of the rabbi's wife.

Tova and I are together as I pace the floor, awaiting the grilling by the Beit Din. Finally, the door opens a crack and they ask me to come in.

I quickly realize my nervousness was unnecessary. This Beit Din is every bit as thorough as in Boston, but the similarities end there. So many questions, so much discussion – but all with a sense of warmth and compassion.

I honestly cannot remember much of what transpired. My hour with them remains a jumbled blur in my mind. All that stands out now is Rabbi Weisfogel's smile and one question he asked me about my singing as an Orthodox Jew, given some of the issues.

Rabbi Weisfogel was born in Ireland, and before World War II studied in the famed Mir Yeshiva in Poland, probably the greatest yeshiva in the world at that time. He escaped Poland just ahead of the Nazis and sought refuge in Shanghai for much of the war.

Now this rabbi, who learned with some of the greatest rabbis of pre-War Europe, is looking at me with a kindly expression as we discuss my singing. His questions are essentially the same ones that were shouted at me on that terrible day with the Boston Beit Din. Ah, but the contrast. Here, there is no shouting. There are no assumptions made – just an open and honest conversation.

The rabbis ask me to step out of the room for the longest ten minutes of my life. When they invite me back, I hear their hearty "Mazel Tov" through a fog, followed by their request that I get ready for the mikveh down the hall.

All this preparation – it's taken years. And now it comes down to this. I descend each step of the mikveh, feeling the water touch my feet and begin to envelop me as I continue down. My eyes take in the white and blue tiles on every side, and I feel the warmth and comfort of this moment surround me.

My feet settle on the floor beyond the last step, three-quarters of me cocooned in the water. I prepare to immerse, conscious that all of me, down to the very last hair, must be covered by the water.

There is only the water – for a brief moment, it is as if nothing else exists. Then I come up, my face hitting the air, jarring me back into the world. I begin to say the blessing for immersing, and when I start to fumble, Tova helps me through it. Then, down into the water two more times. Tova's job is to make sure I immerse fully. She smiles and yells to the rabbis in the next room, "It's good!"

And then I say the Shehechiyanu blessing:

Blessed are You, Lord our God, King of the Universe, Who has given us life, has sustained us, and has brought us to this time.

I woke up this morning simply as Gayle Berman. I've now ascended from the waters of the mikveh reborn as Avigail Shira bat Avraham. Avigail connects to Gayle. I chose Shira as my second name because it means "song." And "bat Avraham " – daughter of Abraham, the appellation given to all converts because we trace our spiritual lineage directly back to Abraham, the first Jew.

But I don't think I feel different. I realize now that I already felt Jewish on the inside. The mikveh was a confirmation of what I've already become.

Love,

Gayle

ॐ∽

October 22, 2006

Dear Gayle,

A part of me says this must be a dream. I grew up in a Reform temple. When I met you, I could barely struggle through the Hebrew alpha-bet, never mind having a clue about what was inside the Hebrew Bible. I went to services on Rosh Hashanah and Yom Kippur and craved lobster the rest of the year. When I met you, you were Minister of Music in a church many times the size of the Monroe Temple, working for a pastor who has since gone on to advise churches around the country how to become mega-churches. We were married by a Justice of the Peace. We said we wouldn't have children.

It's no dream. I couldn't have begun to dream up any of this when we were married sixteen years ago, not even in the wildest recesses of my imagination.

How to understand by what turns of fate it came about that you are an observant Jew, I am an observant Jew, and we are an observant Jewish family. We could just as easily have remained childless. We could just as easily have been sitting together this morning in a Texas mega-church. We could just as easily have a yours-mine-ours situation with church, synagogue, Christmas trees and menorahs wrapped into one not-so-tidy package. We could just as easily have walked away from all religion, touting the ersatz freedom of a life with no strings attached.

But today, it is those possibilities that seem unimaginable. Today, destiny is shouting "observant Jewish family" and nothing else.

But now is not the time to reflect – a big part of the day still beckons. We did manage those two more dunks in the mikveh – you with Ilana and me with Micah – and now we can say everyone in the family is officially Jewish. That transformer action figure and the doll gave them a very positive outlook on the whole thing.

But I can't wait until 6:00 this evening. For at that moment, there will be no more double life – just an Orthodox Jewish family on the inside, on the outside, to everyone. I like the idea that we now need to get married in a Jewish ceremony – it affirms this long trip we've taken together.

I wish we could get married in Springfield, with all our friends cheering us on. But I can't imagine telling everyone that, well actually we haven't exactly been a Jewish family, but now we are, and would they please come to the wedding. Some secrets are best left alone – at least for now.

So we'll get married in front of perfect strangers in Newton. It could be worse. At least we're getting married in Rabbi Samuels' synagogue. Kind of brings it full circle.

In the meantime, the rest of the day has turned out a bit lighter than its profound beginnings. It would have been nice if someone had reminded us before last night that you need a veil and that we need a plain wedding band for the ceremony, unlike what we bought when we got married the first time.

But had we known earlier and had more time to shop, we wouldn't have experienced what it's like to buy a wedding band in the Walmart jewelry department. Nor would we have been so resourceful as to search for a veil among the racks of Halloween costumes at Marshall's. If anyone should comment on the ring or veil, I think I'll just say they're family heirlooms.

Ok – until 6:00. Sixteen years ago, I was blessed to marry a wonderful woman named Gayle. Today, I am blessed to marry Avigail Shira bat Avraham.

Love,

Harold

৵৵

October 22, 2006

Dear Harold,

Real life keeps defying imagination. I imagined we'd have a 20 minute ceremony, eat some food with a few strangers, and drive back to

Springfield. I imagined that my Hebrew teacher Ann, Rabbi Samuels and Rabbi Hyman would be the only people we'd know. When Tova called me last night to ask if I had a veil, I was annoyed that I now had to go on a search when this ceremony, after all, is only "protocol."

Now I understand – this was a real wedding! Rabbi Samuels put out an e-mail to his congregation just a few days ago saying that he needed people to come to the synagogue for a wedding on Sunday evening – and over forty people who didn't know us showed up just like that. Then it turned out that a few knew us after all – Peggy from your old work in Boston, and Michael from my previous work with the Newton schools. Only, they came tonight thinking they were attending an anonymous wedding. How special that Peggy and her husband walked us down the aisle.

Like actors on a movie set, it was as if the director gives the command that the bride and groom sign the ketuba before the ceremony, and the groom has to lift the veil to make sure the right woman is underneath to avoid what happened when Jacob thought he was marrying Rachel but really was marrying Leah (I know it seems far-fetched today, but given how unbelievable everything else has been, I'm sure the mistaken identity thing really has happened to someone, somewhere).

But this wasn't a movie set. It really was my wedding, and the role I was playing was in real life. As I walked down the aisle, I kept blinking, still unable to process that a few dozen people I had never seen before had shown up just to celebrate our special occasion with us.

A few steps later, Rabbi Samuels' and Rabbi Hyman's beaming faces came into view. I decided that these two special people and the strangers holding the chuppah were sent to fulfill one of God's most pleasurable tasks. Micah and Ilana, meanwhile, had no idea what was going on, other than that their parents were getting married (Isn't that supposed to happen before the children?)

My thoughts raced back to our first wedding when friends and family filled the San Antonio Ecumenical Center, and every guest had a personal connection to us. At that time, I had told myself I was going to remain totally aware so that I could later recall each moment.

I had assumed I would never feel the same sense of connection at this wedding, knowing almost no one and with no family in attendance. Little did I imagine that this wedding would become much more meaningful, not only religiously, but communally.

These strangers just showed up. They didn't come because we were family, because they knew us, or had any connection to us. They came to celebrate the wedding of two people, for no other reason than that those two people needed their presence. And some of these strangers even came bearing wedding gifts. A professional musician in the congregation showed up with his keyboard and donated the wedding music (I asked, and he refused to accept any payment). And they all stayed to celebrate with us afterward.

I thought about what kind of a people I am joining. Once, in college, a classmate rejected another student's attempt to convert him to Christianity. The missionary apparently had a nasty tongue, which caused my classmate to ask, "Why would I join with people who talk like that?"

Now I was thinking, why would I not want to join a people who can give of themselves so lovingly and so selflessly? As each rabbi took his turn reflecting on his part in our journey, I kept smiling, determined to hold it together. But when they called up Micah and Ilana, the torrents came rushing from my eyes.

At the party, I remarked to some of the men that when they recited the blessings, they had such big smiles on their faces. One of them said, "When we looked at you, the joy you radiated was palpable. We were just reflecting it back."

Love,

Gayle

––

May 27, 2007

Dear Gayle,

I rarely tire of the view from our front porch, especially on an ideal spring day. The scene looks frozen in time, with Victorians stretching in every direction, in a never-ending parade of Americana. It's easy to understand why they named Springfield the "City of Homes." Other than the cars, I imagine it looks not so different from when Theodore Geisel, a.k.a. "Dr. Suess," was born here a century ago, or when James Naismith invented basketball at the local Y.

Inside the homes, though, a different world prevails today. There is the lawyer, the college professor, the veterinarian, the school teacher – whereas a century ago these homes were the domain mostly of businessmen.

And mostly white businessmen, mostly Christian. Today, our street boasts multiple religions and races. A veritable mirror image of 21st Century America.

Even of 21st Century Jewish America. In the painted lady to our right lives the Katz family – he's Jewish, she's Catholic, kids not raised specifically in either, Christmas tree in the window in December, flag on the porch on the fourth of July.

In the powder green house with the turret to our left live the Blochs – Modern Orthodox, five kids, day school, observe Shabbat, the Torah at the very core of their lives, and about to move to Israel.

And here we sit, smack in the middle. Quite a metaphor for our journey, don't you think?

I can't help but recall a story about Benjamin Disraeli, Britain's Prime Minister in the late 1800s. He was born a Jew, but had been baptized as a boy. Although a Christian, he was always outspoken about his Jewish roots and his affinity for all things Jewish.

Once, the Queen, puzzled by his split identity, asked him, "Who are you and what are you?" Disraeli replied by describing a Christian bible in which there is typically a blank page separating the Old Testament from the New. "I," Disraeli replied, "am that blank page."

Our house is the buffer between these two worlds that are almost stereotypes of the two main turns Jews are taking today. Except that we aren't a blank page. We don't straddle two worlds. We made the long journey from one to the other. Our house didn't move, but it transformed from the one on our right to the one on our left.

The Christian Illinois farm girl is today an Orthodox Jew. The boy from the Monroe Temple of Liberal Judaism who married that farm girl is today an Orthodox Jew. The children born in north-ernmost Arctic Russia are today Orthodox Jews.

I can't begin to understand. I can only be profoundly grateful that we are no longer a blank page, no longer swimming between two poles, no longer balancing the double life of an interfaith family.

We are a Jewish family, not by fate, but by choice, by design and by destiny. We have made this journey together.

And we have come home.

Love,

Harold

ॐ◌

Postscript – March 22, 2010

Dear Harold,

From his tone of voice, I at first thought my father was telling you about the weather they've been having here in Central Illinois and what it means for the crops this year. Sitting in the back of the van, my thoughts slowly turned from my Mom in the nursing home to my Dad's words from the front seat. With a jolt, I realized this was no conversation about the weather. As hard as it was to hear from the back, little snippets filtered through.

"Some family genealogical research . . . found the names of family members . . .

on the synagogue rolls . . .

Bremen, Germany."

Love,

Gayle

ॐ◌

Acknowledgements

If it takes a village to raise a child, then it certainly takes a village to create a Jewish family. So many special people have made possible not only this book, but the journey on which it is based.

There couldn't be a Jewish journey without at least a few Rabbis in the picture – in our case, more than a few. We would like to thank Rabbis Fred Hyman, Benjamin Samuels, Yitzchak Zev Rabinowitz, Micha Turtletaub, Eli Glaser, Mendel Gurkow and Joel Schwartzman. The support that made our journey possible, however, is not the exclusive domain of rabbis. We couldn't have done it without the guidance and encouragement of Tova Hyman, Ann Geller, Ann Pava, Shana Schachter and Ahuvah Gray.

A special thank you to Deborah Fineblum, Philip Silverman and Susan Vorhand for reviewing early versions of the manuscript and offering critically needed suggestions that have improved the final version immeasurably.

We are also grateful for the many conversations about our new program, *J-Journey*, with Deborah and Philip, as well as Rabbi Binny Freedman, Rabbi Seth Farber, Rabbi Yitz Greenberg, Sylvia Barak Fishman, Jack Wertheimer, and Harold Grinspoon and Diane Troderman. All have offered fantastic ideas and asked the hard-hitting questions that have helped to shape this new program that will provide mentoring and resources to the intermarried family who is interested in making the journey to becoming a traditional Jewish family. (See more about *J-Journey* at the end of the book.)

If we were to thank everyone who deserves it, we would need to fill another book. So, thank you to everyone who has helped us, in ways big and small and in ways you may never know. Whether a delicious Shabbat lunch, help finding our place in the service, a gentle smile, patiently answering an obvious question, or just being a wonderful example to emulate, you have made our path smoother.

Finally, and most important, we owe a debt of gratitude we can never fully repay to our parents: Jack Berman, Arlyne Berman, Audrey Redlingshafer and John Redlingshafer (of blessed memory). You believed in us and gave us the freedom to become who we were meant to be. And to our children: Micah and Ilana. Every day, you bring light into our lives and give us renewed confidence in the future. And to the Holy One, Blessed be He, who has given us everything we have, has sustained us and has brought us to this time and place. It is our fervent prayer that, with His help, this book and the *J-Journey* project can offer inspiration, hope and support to other families who are looking to find their place among the Jewish people.

Glossary

Baptism a central Christian ritual utilizing water to mark the entry of an infant or adult into the Christian faith.

Beit Din a rabbinical court, with the authority to rule over a wide range of religious issues, including conversion.

Breslov Hassidim adherents to the Breslov sect of Hassidic Judaism (which is a form of Orthodox Judaism). Rabbi Nachman of Breslov (1772-1810) was a great-grandson of the Baal Shem Tov, the founder of Hasidism. The Breslov approach stresses joy and simplicity in serving God.

Brit Milah "covenant of circumcision." Brit Milah is the ceremony in which a Jewish boy is circumcised at eight days old (or later when that is not possible). Brit Milah is required of all Jewish males, and is a prerequisite for conversion.

Chabad one of the largest movements within Hassidic Judaism. Chabad is renowned for its successful outreach efforts to Jews worldwide, with a network of over 3,500 synagogues, schools and community centers in over 1,000 cities.

Challah a special braided bread eaten at meals on Shabbat and the Jewish holidays. Each meal begins with two loaves, commemorating the double portion of manna the Torah describes falling before Shabbat when the Israelites traveled through the desert.

Chavurah a small gathering of Jews for the purpose of prayer, study, and lifecycle and social events. The Chavurah movement was especially popular during the 1960s and 1970s, and often provides an alternative to established religious institutions or services.

Communion a central Christian sacrament, based on a central story in the Christian bible, in which the participant eats bread and drinks wine, meant to symbolize (or in certain denominations, actually become) the body and blood of Jesus.

Conservative Judaism see *Jewish Movements*.

Dayeinu a popular Passover song and important part of the Passover Seder. The song consists of a series of verses recounting each miracle performed from the Exodus from Egypt through the building of the Temple in Jerusalem.

Hagaddah the text read during the Passover Seder, primarily recounting the story of the Exodus from Egypt. The Maxwell House Haggadah, referred to in *Doublelife*, was first produced by Maxwell House Coffee in the 1920s, and became a cultural icon.

High Holidays the central Jewish holidays of Rosh Hashanah and Yom Kippur.

Jewish Movements similar to the concept of denominations in Christianity, movements in Judaism are organizational entities with member congregations, educational institutions and a particular theological approach. The primary Jewish movements are:

Orthodox Judaism technically not a movement, but an underlying approach that encompasses several movements. Orthodox Judaism understands the Torah to be of Divine origin and the Torah's commandments binding on every Jew.

Reform Judaism a movement that began in Germany in the 1800s, breaking from the mainstream Orthodox Judaism of its time and instituting sweeping changes in Jewish ritual and theology. The Reform movement views the commandments of the Torah as non-binding guidelines, and instead focuses on individual choice.

Conservative Judaism a middle ground approach between Reform and Orthodox. The Conservative movement initially developed as a reaction to what some saw as the excesses of Reform Judaism, and attempted to "conserve" Jewish ritual and tradition, while still taking a more liberal approach than Orthodox Judaism.

Reconstructionist Judaism a 20th century American movement based on the ideas of Mordechai Kaplan. Jewish law is not considered binding, but a cultural resource to be upheld absent a reason to abandon it.

Kaddish a central prayer of the Jewish liturgy. Different versions of the Kaddish prayer serve different functions in the service. People in mourning and on the anniversary of a loved one's death, say the Mourner's Kaddish, which despite its name, contains no reference to death, but only to the sanctification of God's name.

Kashrut the Hebrew term referring to the Jewish dietary laws as described in the Torah and other Jewish texts.

Kiddush the sanctification prayer over wine recited at the beginning of meals on Shabbat and the Jewish holidays. Kiddush can also refer generically to a gathering after the service that includes food and the prayer over wine.

Kippah a circular head covering worn by observant Jewish men and indicating reverence for God. Also called *yarmulke*.

Kol Nidre the prayer that begins the Yom Kippur eve service, and sets the tone for the entire holiday. Even though the prayer itself is formulaic, it often engenders intense emotions, making the Kol Nidre service the most well-attended in the Jewish calendar.

Mechitza a partition that separates men and women during Orthodox prayer services. The mechitza, according to the Talmud, originated in the Temple in Jerusalem, where there was a balcony for women.

Messianic Judaism a form of Christianity. Theologically indistinguishable from evangelical forms of Christianity, Messianic Judaism attempts to convince Jews to become Christians while still maintaining a veneer of Jewish identity and culture.

Mezuzah a piece of parchment, usually housed in a decorative casing, and attached to a Jewish home's exterior and interior door frames. The parchment is inscribed with the Shema and other verses from the book of Deuteronomy, in accordance with Biblical instruction.

Mikveh a natural or specially created body of water used for ritual immersion in Judaism. The construction of the mikveh must adhere to specific requirements and has several uses, including immersion for conversion.

Minyan a Jewish prayer quorum. A minyan requires a minimum of ten, without which certain prayers (such as the Kaddish) may not be said and the Torah may not be publicly read.

Modeh Ani a short prayer said by Jews immediately upon arising – "I thank You, living and eternal King, for restoring my soul in mercy. Great is Your faithfulness."

Oneg Shabbat a Shabbat gathering, usually with refreshments. In Reform Judaism, the reception after Friday night services is called *Oneg Shabbat* or simply *Oneg. Oneg* means *delight.*

Oral Law Judaism traditionally understands that the revelation at Mount Sinai, in addition to the written Torah, included instructions given verbally that supply more details about how to observe the Torah, and without which the written details would be insufficient. The Oral Law was codified in the Mishna in 200 C.E. and was further elucidated in subsequent commentaries.

Orthodox Judaism see *Jewish Movements.*

Parshat Mikeitz The Torah is divided into weekly sections. Each section, called a *parsha*, is named, usually with one of the first Hebrew words of the section. Parshat Mikeitz, mentioned in *Doublelife,* is from the book of Genesis and includes a part of the Joseph story.

Reconstructionist Judaism see *Jewish Movements.*

Reform Judaism see *Jewish Movements.*

Seder the retelling of the Exodus story on the eve of Passover. Meaning *order*, the Seder follows an established pattern, detailed in the Haggadah.

Seder Plate a special plate displayed at the Seder, containing six items, each relating to the Exodus story.

Shabbat/Shabbos the Hebrew word for the Sabbath. Jews often extend a special Sabbath greeting, either *Good Shabbos* or *Shabbat Shalom.*

Shofar traditionally made from a ram's horn and sounded on Rosh Hashana, Yom Kippur, the month preceding Rosh Hashana and certain other occasions.

Sukkah a temporary hut that stands during the week-long holiday of Sukkot, as described in the Torah. The Sukkah holds several symbolic meanings, and Jews traditionally eat and sleep in the Sukkah during the holiday.

Sukkot the Biblical holiday following Yom Kippur and taking place in the fall.

Yeshiva a Jewish school where students learn traditional religious texts such as the Torah and the Talmud.

Tallis/Tallit a Jewish prayer shawl worn during the morning service and certain other times. The tallit includes special fringes, called *tzitzit*, attached to each of its four corners as described in the Torah.

Torah Portion see *Parshat Mikeitz*.

Resources for Your Own Journey of Hope

Thousands of people have converted to Judaism. Thousands of interfaith couples have become Jewish families. But many thousands more are waiting in the wings, not sure where to turn or how to access traditional Judaism, looking for the friendly voice and supportive environment that will help move them forward.

The solution is *J-Journey*.

J-Journey is a new resource for interfaith families who are interested in exploring traditional Judaism. *J-Journey* will offer what has never been offered before – the opportunity to work with couples who began as interfaith but have made the journey to becoming observant Jewish families. For the first time, interfaith families who want to explore becoming observant Jewish families will be able to consult with people who once stood in their shoes and have made the journey they now want to take.

You can begin your own journey at *www.j-journey.org*. You'll find:

- *Friendly Advice* – You can use our *Ask a Rabbi* feature to post questions about Jewish observance and conversion to a rabbi with years of experience working with converts. Or you can choose our *Ask a Friend* feature to pose more personal questions (such as family issues, dealing with parents, obstacles encountered on the way) to someone who has made the journey from interfaith to Jewish and can assist based on personal experience.

- *Helpful Information* – You can browse our regularly updated resource list, featuring the best books, web sites, blogs and practical information to inspire and inform you on your journey.

- *An Inspiring Community* – You can become part of the conversation on our blog (also available at **www.doublelifejourney.com**), which tackles cutting-edge Jewish issues and features guest bloggers who share their own stories about embracing Judaism. You can also sign up to connect with a personal mentor who has already traveled the path from interfaith to Jewish.

If you are an *interfaith family interested in becoming an observant Jewish family*, come to j-journey.org to get the assistance and inspiration you need.

If you are an *observant Jewish family who began as interfaith*, come to j-journey.org to find out how you can join our mentor network and help others take the journey you already have.

If you are a *Jewish family*, refer j-journey.org to relatives and friends who may be able to benefit from our resources. Or simply follow the conversation to draw inspiration for your own Jewish practice.

www.j-journey.org

Bring the Authors To Your Community

If you have questions, comments, or would like Harold and Gayle to speak, or lead a workshop for your community or organization, please visit www.doublelifejourney.com.